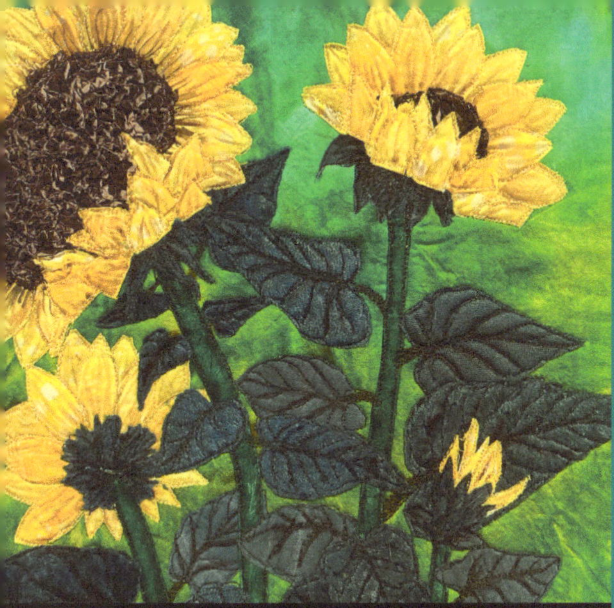

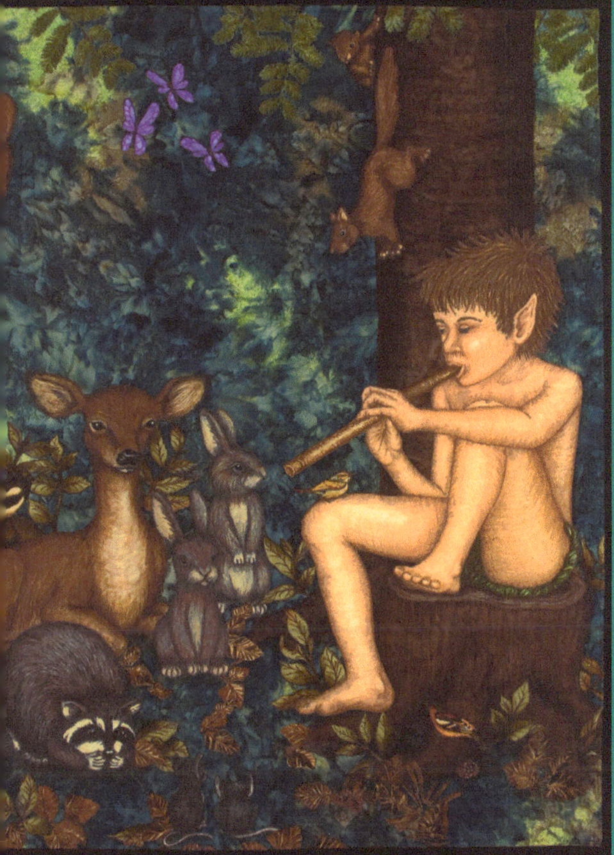

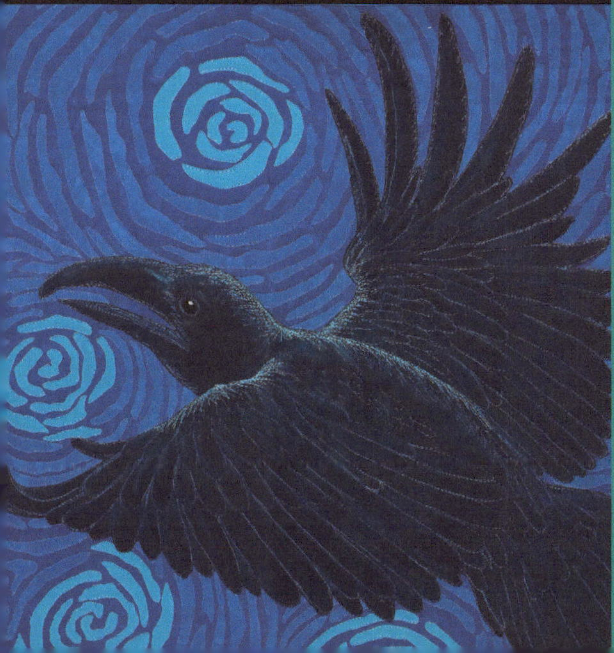

# Pigment Patchwork

## Artful Techniques for Fabric Embellishment

## Rhonda Denney

**Emporia, Kansas**

**Pigment Patchwork: Artful Techniques for Fabric Embellishment**
by Rhonda Denney



www.RhondaDenney.com

Published by: Cap Rock Inspirations (CRI) Press, PO Box 741, Emporia KS 66801

Cover designer: Nick Zelinger, NZ Graphics

Library of Congress Control Number: 2022914510

Softcover ISBN 978-0-9969093-1-0

eBook ISBN 978-0-9969093-2-7

Printed in the United States of America

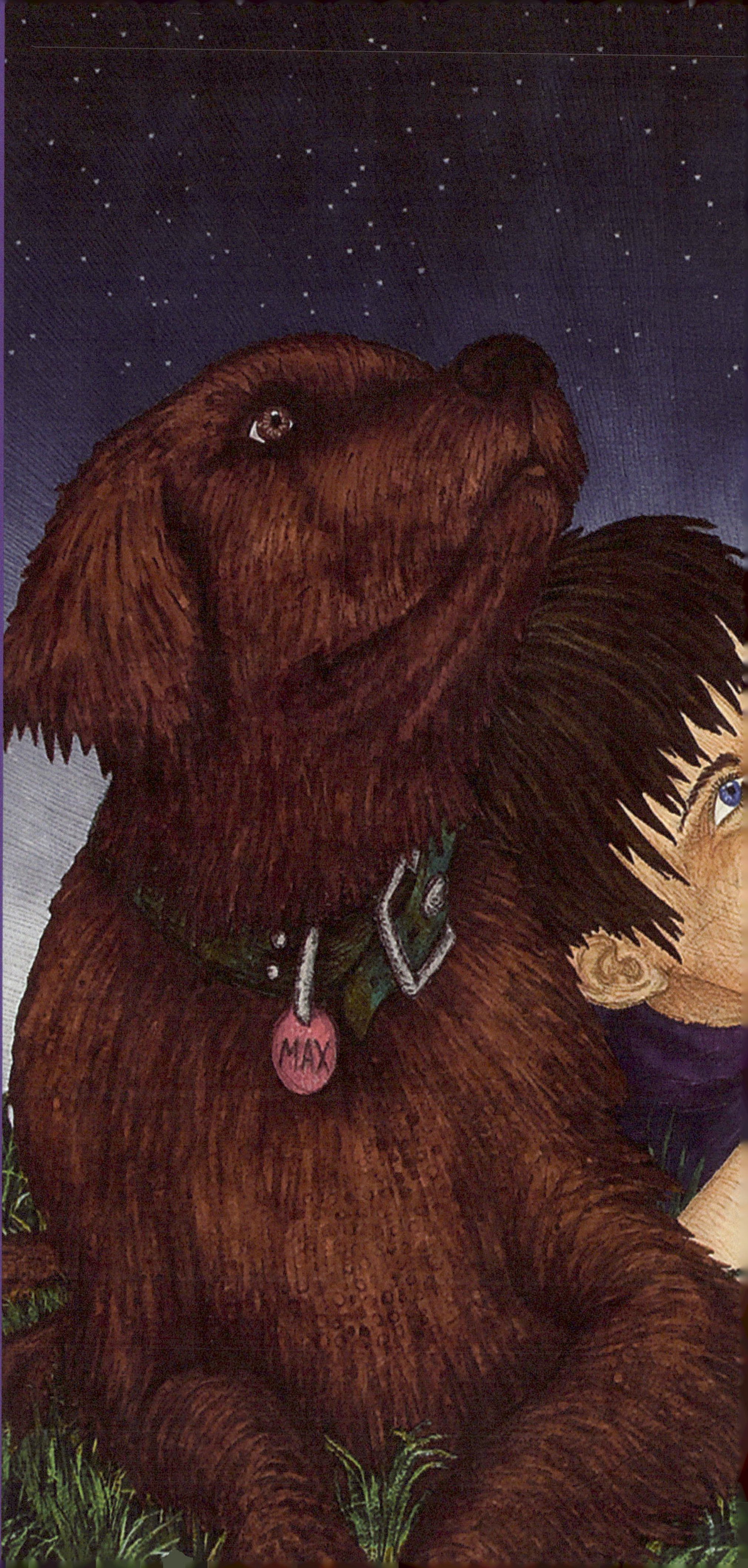

## Acknowledgments

To Raymond A. Fallen, my husband. What can I say? You are my rock, supporting and encouraging me from the very beginning of my Pigment Patchwork journey. You continually stepped in to take up the slack with house and animal chores when creating this book took over my life. We have a wonderful partnership, one that has lasted for 27 years. Our relationship is give and take and we make it work, especially because we have rescued animals that need our help and care. Thank you Ray.  Love you.

To my dear friends Elda Kohls and Fern Hill. Both ladies were supporters and inspiration to me. Both are no longer here, but are forever in my heart. I know you would be proud of this book.

Thank you to Jim West, owner of Craftours, a niche market travel agency, for helping me brainstorm the term "Pigment Patchwork" to describe my techniques.

Thank you to Shelly Heesacker, producer of The Quilt Show, for throwing down the challenge to create this book, something I had been thinking about doing for years. You knew what it took to motivate me!

For many of the ideas behind the content of this book, I want to thank all my friends  and students who attended my workshops on my techniques. I learned from each and every one of you. Watching you enjoy learning about using pigments on fabric; helping me hone my teaching skills; as well as giving me feedback, ideas and suggestions for topics or changes. This book is another way for me to reach out so others can gain confidence in their own abilities and potential.

A special thank you to renowned quilter Ricky Tims for writing the foreword and back cover testimonial. We have been connected in many different ways throughout the years I have been involved with quilting and fiber art. It means so much that you recognize my growth as an art quilter.

It takes a dedicated team to put a book together. Mike Daniels, The Publisher's Coach, helped encourage and guide the process. Nick Zelinger, NZ Graphics, the book cover designer, helped design the interior. Thank you both.

To my friends and family who gave feedback on the book contents, I am ever so grateful! Your investment of time and energy was much appreciated. Each of you brought your own expertise into play and this book is so much better for that.

Ray Fallen
Gail Denney McGowan
Robyn Denney Riggs
Jenae Redmond
Mary Lee Mahr
Deane Hay

# Contents


Acknowledgments . . . . . . . . . . . . . . . . . . . . . . . . . iii

Foreword . . . . . . . . . . . . . . . . . . . . . . . . . . . . 1

The Journey . . . . . . . . . . . . . . . . . . . . . . . . . . 3

Tips & Advice . . . . . . . . . . . . . . . . . . . . . . . . 11

   Time Commitment . . . . . . . . . . . . . . . . . . . . 11

   Tips for Organizing your Notes to Maximize your
      Learning . . . . . . . . . . . . . . . . . . . . . . 11

   Workspace . . . . . . . . . . . . . . . . . . . . . . . . 12

   Lighting . . . . . . . . . . . . . . . . . . . . . . . . . 13

   Stabilizing your Fabric - Options . . . . . . . . . . . . 14

   How to Iron your Fabric onto Freezer Paper (FP) . . . . 15

   Pigment Permanency on Fabric . . . . . . . . . . . . 16

   How to Heat-Set Pigments on Fabric Using a Dry Iron . 17

   Cleaning Up After Using Pigments . . . . . . . . . . . 18

Tools and Supply List . . . . . . . . . . . . . . . . . . . 21

   Your Assignment - Tools and Supply List . . . . . . . . 21

Part 1 - My Approach . . . . . . . . . . . . . . . . . . . 23

   Using this Book . . . . . . . . . . . . . . . . . . . . . 23

   Rhonda's 8-week Get Pigment Confident (GPC)
      Challenge . . . . . . . . . . . . . . . . . . . . . . 23

   My Goal with this Book . . . . . . . . . . . . . . . . . 24

   Why Do I Use Patterns for the Exercises in this Book? . 24

   Words of Inspiration . . . . . . . . . . . . . . . . . . 25

Part 2 - Getting Aquainted - Lets Color . . . . . . . 27

   Introduction to Derwent Inktense Pencils . . . . . . . 27

   Supplies Needed for this Exercise . . . . . . . . . . . 27

   Pattern for Let's Color! - Butterflies . . . . . . . . . . 28

   Let's Color! Part 1 - Color on Fabric Alone . . . . . . . 28

   Let's Color! Part 2 - Color on Stabilized Fabric . . . . . 30

   Let's Color! Part 3 - Fixing Pigments on Fabric Using
      Dry Heat . . . . . . . . . . . . . . . . . . . . . . 31

   Summary - Getting Acquainted - Let's Color! . . . . . 31

Part 3 - Essential Elements - Pigments & Fabric 35

   Why Essential? . . . . . . . . . . . . . . . . . . . . . 35

What is Pigment? . . . . . . . . . . . . . . . . . . . . . . . . . . 35

Commercial Manufacturing of Pigments . . . . . . . . . . . . . . 40

Basics of Fabric . . . . . . . . . . . . . . . . . . . . . . . . . . . 48

Summary - Essentials - Pigments and Fabric . . . . . . . . . . . 53


## Part 4: Techniques & Tools: Getting Ready . . . . . . . . . 55


Getting Ready to Use Pigments on Your Fabric . . . . . . . . . 55

Decisions Before you Start Your Project . . . . . . . . . . . . . 56

Considerations in Using Pigments on Fabric . . . . . . . . . . . 57

Let's Experiment . . . . . . . . . . . . . . . . . . . . . . . . . . 58

Test Using Section 1 of the Test Sheet . . . . . . . . . . . . . . 61

More Experimenting - Section 2 . . . . . . . . . . . . . . . . . . 65

Experiment Specific to Your Project - Section 3 . . . . . . . . . 67

Reflections on Your Testing . . . . . . . . . . . . . . . . . . . . 69

## Part 4: Techniques & Tools: Let's Start Your Project . . . . 71


Reflections . . . . . . . . . . . . . . . . . . . . . . . . . . . . . . 71

Before You Start Your Project – More Decisions . . . . . . . . . 71

Start Your Design . . . . . . . . . . . . . . . . . . . . . . . . . . 74

Get Ready to Begin . . . . . . . . . . . . . . . . . . . . . . . . . 79

Are We There Yet? Am I Done? . . . . . . . . . . . . . . . . . . 81

Your Assignment - Start Coloring on Your First Project . . . . . 81


## Part 4: Techniques & Tools: Look What I Created! . . . . . 82


A Project Ready to Review . . . . . . . . . . . . . . . . . . . . . 82

Looking Back - Successes and Challenges . . . . . . . . . . . . 82

Summary – Reviewing your Project Using a 4-step
Analysis Process . . . . . . . . . . . . . . . . . . . . . . . . . . 85

Your Assignment - Reflect and Analyze . . . . . . . . . . . . . . 85


## Part 4: Techniques & Tools: Can I Fix It? . . . . . . . . . . . 86


Adjusting Your Piece - Potential Alternatives . . . . . . . . . . . 86

Your Assignment (optional) - Adjust things you don't like in
your project . . . . . . . . . . . . . . . . . . . . . . . . . . . . 92


## Where to From Here . . . . . . . . . . . . . . . . . . . . . . . . 95


Finishing Your Learning Assignment Project . . . . . . . . . . . 95

Tips on Finishing Your Project . . . . . . . . . . . . . . . . . . . 95

## Some Final Thoughts & Words of Wisdom . . . . . . . . . 109

Your Creative Voice - What Is It? . . . . . . . . . . . . . 109

Your Creative Voice - How to Find It . . . . . . . . . . . 109

Where to Now? . . . . . . . . . . . . . . . . . . . . . . . . 109

Final Words of Wisdom . . . . . . . . . . . . . . . . . . . 110

## Highlights of Some of Rhonda's Work . . . . . . . . . . . . . 113

*Zebra - The Eyes Have It (TEHI)* . . . . . . . . . . . . . 114

*Hans my Hedgehog* . . . . . . . . . . . . . . . . . . . . . 116

*How Sweet It Is ... Buzzing with Bees* . . . . . . . . . . 120

*Rabbit - Winter Early Morning Light* . . . . . . . . . . . 124

*Rub-a-dub-dub* – Pieces of the Past . . . . . . . . . . . 126

Summary - Highlights of Some of Rhonda's Work . . . . . . . 130

## Templates, Patterns and Reference Materials . . . . . . . . 133

Butterflies Line Pattern - 2 patterns to a page Overview . . . . 133

Test Sheet Templates - Generic Overview . . . . . . . . . . . . 133

Koi Fish Line Pattern and Reference Materials - Overview . . . 133

Deer Portrait Line Pattern and Reference Materials - Overview . 133

Color Wheel Reference Materials - Overview . . . . . . . . . 133

BECOME A PIGMENT TRAILBLAZER!
Pigment Patchwork

# Foreword

by Ricky Tims, renowned quilter, author, teacher, and co-host of TheQuiltShow.com

Rhonda Denney first came into my world when she attended a quilt retreat I was presenting in the small town of La Veta, Colorado. She was one of those thoughtful and diligent students who wanted to make the most of the days she was there. Afterwards, she began searching for her creative voice - exploring many techniques and styles. As a stand-out student, I took note and continued to follow her quilting journey - even acquiring some of her early small works which had been displayed in my gallery. Soon her quilts were winning prizes in regional shows. Subsequently, she has won awards at high profile international quilt competitions.

Pigment Patchwork is a culmination of years of Rhonda's growth, trials, triumphs, failures, and successes. The information she provides herein will motivate you to try new techniques and guide you to create realistic designs in your own quilts. I am proud to have been part of her quilting journey, but assure all of you, she has achieved much because of her own passion, diligence, and love for the quilting arts.

## The Journey

I consider myself a 'late bloomer' when it comes to sewing and fiber art.

Although I always loved to draw and enjoyed it as a creative outlet, sewing and other artistic pursuits did not fit into my young life as a tomboy who preferred to climb trees or engage in other similar adventures.  As a young adult, I went on to complete my college education, earning an Associate Degree during my three-year enlistment in the Army, a bachelor's degree in computer science and later a master's degree in systems management. My first job was in the Information Technology (IT) sector, which I combined with service in the United States Army Reserve (USAR). My career choices did not leave me time for much else.

I retired from the USAR in 2000 and, with guidance from a friend and the encouragement of my husband, I purchased a bed-quilt kit that appealed to me. So, with my new Bernina Quilters Edition sewing machine and some basic supplies, I began my journey into quilting atop my kitchen table.  This Trip Around the

World pattern kit, using wonderful hand-dyed fabrics, was my first project.  Though the quilt top, with the addition of my own columbine flower appliqués for the quilt corners, was completed in several months, it took me several years to finish the quilt itself as I practiced and became more proficient with quilting. I call this quilt *Trip Around the Rockies*. As I learned more, I realized that art quilting was more my style.

A good friend recommended that I take a color class from Heather Thomas in 2004 to expand my knowledge. That class showed me that I could "get out of the box" with my design techniques. That was all the encouragement I needed! Although I wish I'd spent time learning more about sewing growing up, that lack of knowledge allowed me to consider other ways of creating with fabrics.

In 2004, my husband and I moved to a beautiful, remote piece of land northwest of Canon City, Colorado, and built our dream home. I was able to work part-time remotely, which allowed me to assist in our home building process. After helping the crew build the house structure, we did most of the rest of the work ourselves.  Soon after, I officially left work to live on the ranch. We lived off-grid, using solar power, with a well and septic system. It was a 26-mile one-way drive to pick up mail and shop for groceries.

Our only access to the internet was through a satellite connection, and it was the only way our cell phones worked. We were so remote that Global Positioning Systems (GPS) could not find us on the map. My creative time with art quilts was limited because we were focused on building our house and taking care of chores. I did finish my Heather Thomas color class, but I

had to stay weekends with a friend in Boulder, Colorado, in order to use her sewing room to complete my assignments.

In 2005, I took a Faces in Fabric class from Lura Schwarz Smith at a quilt store in Denver, Colorado. That class introduced me to textile inks, opening the doors to more creativity. I started thinking about other pigments that I could use on fabric.

In 2006, a chance reconnection with my grade school art teacher reignited my interest in art. She introduced me to some techniques she used for using

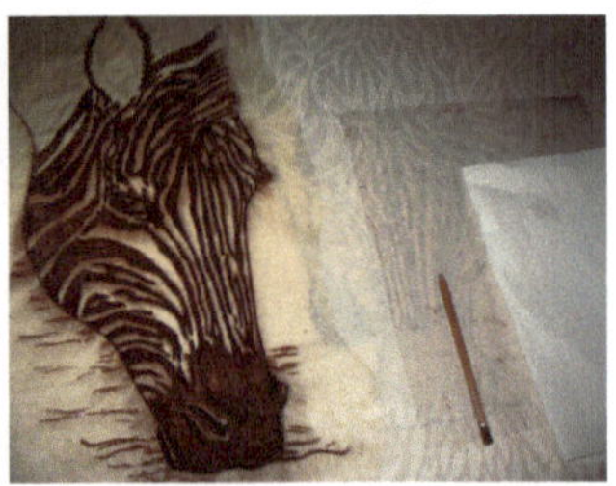

pigments on fabric. I got very excited with the possibilities. I created my first pieces using pastels on silk noil treated with a special formula to make the pigment permanent. I also used color pencils on silk stretched in a hoop.

From that beginning, I continued to explore and experiment. I wanted to simplify the process and look at other ways to use pigments to color on fabric. Because of our location, my closest art quilting friends were at least a 1½-hour drive away. That, combined with limited internet, pushed me to try things on my own. I loved being motivated by quilting Calls for Entry and Challenges.

In March 2007, I attended a Ricky Tims retreat in La Veta, Colorado, my first ever quilting

retreat. Justin Shults offered a Fabric Dyeing Workshop at the same location a few days before the retreat. I played with using pigments on the fabric during the retreat, using them for my projects. At the retreat I heard about Ricky's Call for Entries for his upcoming quilt challenge called MicroCosmos: Little Worlds. The theme was Yesterday, Today, and Tomorrow. Entries were a triptych, three separate miniatures, improvisational works, each measuring exactly 5 x 7 inches.

It was a very short window, but I was inspired, so I went home and started designing. I had so much fun that I submitted three separate entries. Two of my entries were juried into the show, with the third placed in the gift shop.

I attended the opening night and was very excited to see that my *Hope After Maelstrom – Wildfire* triptych won the Excellence in Innovation award. I met the show judge and talked with him. It felt like my feet weren't even touching the ground! To top it off, I also won the People's Choice award for that same triptych! Two of the three triptychs sold. The third, *Western Heritage - Longhorns*, is very special to me because it reminds me of our ranch. That

experience built my confidence tremendously and I was galvanized to continue exploring.

In 2011, I went on an organized guided tour trip to Nairobi, Kenya, East Africa organized by Craftours, a niche market travel company. During the Safari game drives, we were organized into small groups of six people. During these rides, we decided to create a Round Robin quilt project so each of us would

have a souvenir of the trip. I had never done a Round Robin quilt, but I was willing to try! For this project, I used my

pigments to create colored sketches of some of the animals we saw during our safaris. I learned a lot from this project. In fact, every time I use my pigments to color on fabric, I learn more about it.

In 2012, I discovered a wonderful group, the Westcliffe Art Quilters (WAQ) in Westcliffe, Colorado. We met each month. This was a chance to connect with people wanting to explore creativity with fiber art quilts. I only wish I had found the group sooner.

When I was invited to join them, the group was in the middle of a year-long project. They called it "12 x 12." They had 12 topic words. Each month they were to create a 12" x 12" art quilt using one of the topic words. At the end of the twelve months, each person would have a total of 12 pieces. We were encouraged to try a variety of surface design and quilting techniques on these.

I was in heaven! The pieces were small enough that I could catch up and meet the deadline, but large enough to really think about and try different techniques. At the end of the project, the WAQ group pieces were displayed together, organized by topic name, on black felt. It was a magnificent exhibit of imagination and creativity! I was hooked on continuing to develop my techniques.

Why do I call my techniques "Pigment Patchwork"? I have my friend Jim West of Craftours to thank for that. I showed him some of my original work while on a Craftours trip to China. Jim told me that he had never seen anything like my work and techniques and suggested I come up with a name to identify them. So, while traveling on a tour bus on the way to the Great Wall of China, we brainstormed and came up with "Pigment Patchwork."

Since then, I have continued to hone my skills using pigments. Friends wanted to know how I created my pieces and asked me to teach them, so I created my workshops. I have always loved teaching, sharing ideas and comparing notes. Over the years I continue learning and sharing.

My biggest challenge with workshops was the limited time participants had to really explore, understand, and experience using pigments on fabric. So, I created an 8-week ***Get Pigment Confident (GPC) Challenge*** to educate people on the details of my approach and methods. That was a definite move in the right direction.

My friends encouraged me to write a book about my techniques, allowing me to reach more people. The book is meant to be stand alone for learning or, if you want support and encouragement along the way, it can be combined with my 8-week GPC Challenge so I can personally amplify your learning experience. I am so excited that you are here. Have fun!

Rhonda Denney

2000 to Present

Pigment
Patchwork

# Pigment Patchwork Concepts

Pigment Patchwork is a set of techniques I developed over the years through experimentation with pigments and stitching on all kinds of fabric. It has grown into a philosophy that allows me to approach any project that uses pigments and stitching with confidence. Learning about pigments and their effect allows me to maximize their use in my artwork. It is always a learning experience. As a result, my creative voice continues to grow. My work is a dance between the pigments and me on the fabric. With the addition of stitching, my work develops even more dimensionality and depth.

The Pigment Patchwork philosophy embraces:

- A sense of adventure, mystery, and discovery
- A willingness to experiment using different techniques and methods of creation, learning as you go
- The development and enrichment of your own creative voice
- The interplay of pigments on fabric and stitching to enhance the design, providing dimension and accentuating form
- A pleasing and challenging partnership with your creative side

# Tips and Advice

## Tips & Advice

I know you're excited to just jump in, but when working with color mediums, there are some precautions and lessons I've learned during my own journey that will save you time and money, and help to contain the pigments to your workspace. These tips will help you make the most of your creative time and learning opportunities.

My advice is organized into the following topics:

TIPS

- Your time commitment to the Learning Assignments in this book

- Tips for organizing your notes to maximize your learning

- Your workspaces

- Lighting

- Stabilizing your fabric to color on it using pigments - options

- How to stabilize fabric using freezer paper

- Permanency and stability of pigments on fabric

- How to heat-set pigments on fabric using an iron

- Cleaning up after using pigments

### *Time Commitment*

This book is structured into sections and components that can be read at your own speed based on the time that you have. It is difficult to assign or recommend a specific amount of time.  The book has been organized so it can be used as a reference tool even after you have gone through the Learning Activities.

You are in total control of your learning journey. The Learning Activities will require time to work on your own project, following the associated instructions. How long that takes is up to you. And you are not limited to only the suggested project; you can invest more time and explore other aspects related to that assignment.  The instructions will outline that more as you move through the book.

### *Tips for Organizing your Notes to Maximize your Learning*

The following sections are in outline format; it is an easier way to present my recommendations.

### Tips and Recommendations to Maximize your Learning

- Keep your camera handy and use it

- Write or dictate notes about what is happening; don't depend on your memory; write enough detail so you will be able to jog your memory later

- Set up a system early and start using it consistently

### Keeping Good Records and Notes - What to Document?

- This book's activities and your projects -

  - Step-by-step photos (these will be invaluable)

  - Notes on likes, dislikes, lessons learned, etc.; sometimes this is a powerful

way to help you remember

- Approach this as pictures/notes for your eyes only; write words, use symbols (emojis, arrows, stars, exclamation points, etc.) that you can identify with

- Be disciplined - you will not regret it

### Setting up a Note System - What is Ideal?

- A Project File, all in one place, with:

  - Step-by-step photos

  - Notes on approach, thoughts, techniques (document directly on your fabric if applicable), etc.

  - Patterns, reference materials, etc.

  - Fabric swatches, etc.

- In a binder or file packet or set of files; build as you go

### Recommendations About Notes and Project Documentation

- Do not make the mistake of thinking you will remember all the details

- Do what works for you; we all learn differently

- Once you see the value in doing something, it becomes easier to remember to do it

- Be kind to yourself; this should be a fun experience, like an adventure

### Your Assignment - Let's Get Organized

You may already have a way of organizing your project documentation. It

may be fine for the kind of fabric projects that you normally create but, unless experimentation is part of your creative process, your current documentation method may not be up to the task. Consider what you are doing now and what changes you should make based on my recommendations.

The progress photos included in this book are intended to serve as an additional tool to explain the Pigment Patchwork process and techniques. My earlier projects were not so well documented, so I had few examples to show. Thankfully I changed my ways and, as a result, had better resources to use for this book. This same lesson applies to you and your journey.

Whatever project documentation method you choose to use, get it organized and ready to go. Then make the commitment to diligently use it.

### *Workspace*

The best workspace for coloring on fabric using pigments should have the following:

- A large, flat, non-textured surface to work on that can be easily covered with plastic or paper, if needed

- Space to lay out all of your supplies so they are within easy reach to use

- A comfortable chair or stool to sit on or, if you stand while working, a comfortable floor surface to lessen leg fatigue

### Safeguarding your Project from Unwanted Pigment

You will be investing your time, pigments, fabric and intentions during your projects. In a nutshell, pigments are defined as finely ground solid particles of colorant that are mixed with a binder of some kind. So, what does that

mean in terms of safeguarding your work area and process?

**Protecting Work Surfaces**

Pigment particles can travel, moving from the location you apply them (by coloring) to other surfaces. They can even move when opening a particular type of pigment, such as a container or marking pen. Plan to use plastic or paper to cover your work surface. Wear old clothing to protect yourself from vagrant pigments. Consider how to protect your project itself during the process.

*Using Parchment Paper to Protect Surfaces*

Parchment paper, also called baking or bakery paper, is a food-safe coated paper used in baking and cooking, and is a good protective tool to use. It is coated with silicone, making it nonstick, grease-proof, and heat-resistant.  Brown parchment is unbleached; white parchment is chemically treated to remove the paper's natural color. Both can be purchased in rolls or cut sheets.

It does not matter what type of parchment paper you use. However, if you are sensitive to chemicals, the unbleached parchment paper is not chlorine treated and is not bleached and, therefore, contains fewer chemicals. Unbleached paper may be healthier and safer than the bleached paper since chemical fumes may be generated by the heat of a hot iron on the parchment paper and can be breathed in.

You can use parchment paper to protect work surfaces, your iron, and ironing surfaces. Pieces of parchment paper can be strategically placed on top of your projects, to protect your hands and areas of the project while coloring on the fabric. You can also use sheets of white paper, but parchment paper is preferablc because, in

most cases, its surface resists picking up and carrying pigment particles.

If you use parchment paper with heat, pigments will tend to stick to it more easily and could be transferred. You need to be aware of this tendency. Pigment residue can lay on the surface and transfer to the next piece of fabric. Check your parchment paper frequently, replacing it as needed to minimize cross-contamination.

Are there things you can use instead of parchment paper or white paper? There are specialty silicone mats available at quilt stores, as well as in retail  stores. Search the internet to find locations to get them. You can wash and reuse these mats, but you need to be diligent and careful as even these mats will pick up pigment particles. Because of the mess of cleaning the mats, you may find it easier to use parchment paper.

*Containing Pigment Particles*

When you are using pigments manufactured as a hand-held applicator, similar to a pencil, you will need to continuously expose pigment in order to color with them. Usually this involves using a sharp knife or pencil sharpener. Consider not only the resulting shavings, but pigment that is released during the sharpening process itself. You should catch and contain the shavings so they do not inadvertently spread and color your project or you. A small container with a secure lid is one handy method for that.

### Lighting

It is best to have natural light to work with. There are many lighting fixtures and lamps that have natural-light features. This allows you to see the pigments at their best.

You should also have a lamp that can direct light onto the area in which you are working, allowing you to see without shadows. Good

lighting also helps you take better photographs to document your work. Don't let your lighting stop you from taking pictures. Photographs are very useful and can always be touched up if necessary. Capturing your project as you work is important.

## *Stabilizing your Fabric - Options*

Fabric can be stabilized in many ways:

- Using freezer paper
- Using your fingers
- Using an embroidery hoop
- Using iron-on paper-backed fusibles
- Using fusible appliqué interfacing
- Using fabric medium

Depending on the circumstances or project, any one of these will help with the process of coloring on fabric using pigments.

### Using Freezer Paper to Stabilize Fabric

Freezer paper (FP) is a heavy-duty paper with a plastic coating on one side only. It is made to use in the kitchen, but quilters have been using it for years for appliqué. There are many different brands of freezer paper available. DO NOT use wax paper! It is not the same thing as freezer paper.

You can also find a heavier, card-stock type of freezer paper. You can use it, but it is better suited for making templates for appliqué projects.

### Pros and Cons of Using Freezer Paper

Advantages of ironing your fabric to a piece of freezer paper (FP):

- The "sandwich" flattens the fabric and provides a stable base on which to apply the pigments
- If the fabric separates from the FP when coloring, use the iron again (with parchment paper protection) to reconnect them (this also helps "set" the pigments)

- FP helps minimize any fabric unraveling or fraying at the edges

- FP removes wrinkles so it is easier to see what you are doing

- FP provides a good stable structure for project documentation and testing results on fabric (you can write your reference notes directly on the fabric or on the paper-backing of the FP)

- The fabric/FP unit is easier to handle and store

Disadvantages to this method:

- Coloring on the fabric/FP sandwich will normally start separating it (simply iron it again to reconnect them)

- The plastic coating of the FP backing retains liquid; be careful not to use a lot of water or other liquids unless that is the effect you want; the following can happen:

  - Pooling of the liquid with more uncontrolled wicking of the pigment

  - The heat and weight of the iron may push the wet pigment further out on the fabric when used to dry the wet area

- For an appliqué piece, the fabric must be separated from the FP and attached using adhesive or fusible; if not careful, you can distort the fabric when doing this

### Using your Fingers to Stabilize Fabric

Use the fingers of one hand to hold the fabric taut while coloring with the other hand.  This can be a very tiring process if you are trying to color large areas. The fabric piece needs to be large enough that you can use this method. This method is useful after a fiber piece has been quilted and you want to add pigment. The sandwiching/quilting helps stabilize the fabric, so using the fingers is easier.

## Using Embroidery Hoops or Stretcher Bars to Stabilize Fabric

Stretch and stabilize your fabric using an embroidery hoop or stretcher bars. Put the fabric into the hoop so you can color flat against your work surface (place your fabric wrong side up so that you turn the hoop over to color). If you are using wet additives to the pigments, you can lift the piece so it is not flat on the work surface and lay it so it can air-dry more quickly.

You will have to take the fabric out of the hoop to iron it to set the color unless the hoop and iron are comparably sized. You will still get wicking using this technique if you use water or any other medium.

## Using Paper-backed Iron-on Fusibles to Stabilize Fabric

Iron-on fusibles can be used as a stabilizer instead of FP, as long as they have a backing paper. When working on a piece that has many different fabrics and/or small pieces of fabric, you may choose to use an iron-on fusible instead of FP. It makes for less handling of tiny pieces of fabric. Just like FP, if the fabric separates from the fusible, use a hot iron to re-adhere them. This works well for delicate fabrics as well.

## Using Fusible Appliqué Backing to Stabilize Fabric

Fusible appliqué backing can also be used to stabilize your fabric. This is usually a white fabric coated with fusible that you iron your fabric onto, giving you a double layer of fabric. This also helps against shadowing when appliquéing on dark fabric. Unless the appliqué backing has fusible on both sides, you will need to fuse or glue the piece onto the final surface.

## Using a Fabric Medium to Stabilize Fabric

You can stabilize fabric by treating it with a medium. The composition of most mediums is a plastic base. When painted or applied to the

fabric, it will make it more stiff, changing the "hand" of the fabric.

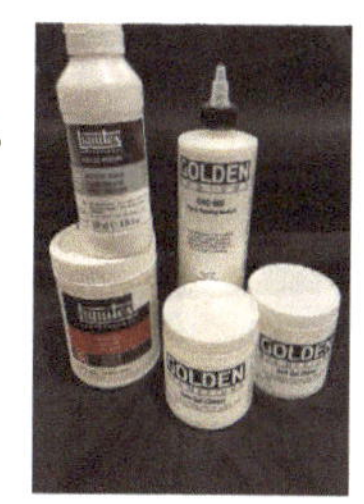

This method of fabric stabilization was used for a project with school children coloring on fabric, using colored pencils only. No liquid medium was used during coloring. The time was limited to a 35-minute class period. To simplify the process, the fabric was stabilized ahead of time and cut to size. The fabric yardage was drenched in a liquid fabric medium and let dry. After ironing, the fabric was cut to size. The results were stiff enough so that no other method of stabilization was needed. This method eliminated the need for hot irons in the classrooms.

Note: There was no stitching done on top of these fabric "blocks." If there had been, the stitching holes may have remained visible because of the hand of the fabric. This is something you should consider if you want to use this method.

## Last Thoughts on Stabilizing Your Fabric

Six different methods to stabilize your fabric have been covered. There may be others. Don't ever underestimate the ingenuity of need. After all, they say that "necessity is the mother of invention." If you have other methods that have worked well for you, I would love to hear about them!

## *How to Iron your Fabric onto Freezer Paper (FP)*

It is recommended that you use the FP method to stabilize your fabric for the Learning Activities in this book. If you have never ironed fabric to FP before, refer to the instructions below.

1.  Use a pre-heated iron (med-high, no steam).

2.  Place FP (cut the same size as your fabric) on your ironing surface with the plastic side

(shiny) up. You may also want to lay parchment paper down to protect your ironing surface.

3. Place your fabric on top of the FP (wrong side of fabric down), lining it up carefully.

4. Optional: Place parchment paper on top of fabric (see photo) to protect iron.



5. Place iron on top of the stack and hold there for 15 to 20 seconds. Lift the iron off and check to see if the fabric is sticking to the FP. If not, lay the iron on top for 10 seconds more, then check again and again. Move the iron to another spot and continue. You want the fabric to adhere to the FP consistently across its surface.

6. Lift iron and set aside. Check the fabric to see if the sandwich is sticking together. If not, or if there are sections not sticking, repeat the previous step until all is secure.

## CAUTION!

- Do not use steam! It may cause injury!

- Surfaces may get hot! Don't burn your fingers!

- The use of parchment paper to protect your iron and ironing surfaces is always recommended

- Wear an overshirt to protect your clothing; pigment can travel

## Tips!

- You can re-adhere your fabric to the FP many times over; re-ironing helps keep your surface stabilized (FP will not last forever doing this, but it will last a long time)

- Burning FP or fabric by overheating with the iron is unlikely, so don't be afraid of this; if the paper starts smoking or

turning brown, your iron is too hot; turn the heat down

- When you use parchment paper to protect your surfaces, check it to see how much pigment remains behind on it after use; replace with a clean sheet when the parchment paper gets dirty with pigment; otherwise, you may find pigment traveling and potentially staining everything

- Suggestion: To make it easy to store your fabric/FP testing sheets and projects, trim them to 8" x 10"; slide them into a page protector for easy storage and access; or fold larger pieces to store in page protectors; store filled page protectors in 3-ring binders

## Pigment Permanency on Fabric

The challenge in covering this topic is dealing with different terms and their definitions. Words such as "permanence," "lightfastness," "archivability" and "fastness" are used when discussing art. Regardless of the surface you are using, these terms apply. Your understanding may affect your choice of pigments to use.

### Terms Defined

### Permanence

The term "permanence of color" signifies the efficiency and quality of the color in terms of its chemical stability.

### Lightfastness

Christopher Derant explains Lightfastness in an online blog at the Ken Bromley Art Supplies Blog:

"Lightfastness is simply how the pigment of the art materials you are using interact with light itself and it is a measurement of a pigment's ability to resist fading or discolouration under normal circumstances. This can be any type of sunlight or ultraviolet light. . . Some pigments can fade in weeks if they are extremely poor and other poor ones can even take up to a year.

The length of exposure, and strength of the light also affect how fast fading can occur."

### Archivability

When artists say "archival," it usually means "durable to the standards of permanent art." Dyes tend to remain colorfast only so long. Pigments, on the other hand, tend to be permanently colorfast, bright, and durable.

### Fastness

Fastness can be defined as the resistance of a piece of fabric colored with pigment to change its characteristics of color. This includes transferring pigment particles to other surfaces (what I call traveling). Fastness is also associated with fading (the color changes and lightens) or bleeding (transferring of the color to another material).

### Should I Care?

Coloring on fabric is not permanent as dyeing fabric is, even after the pigments are "set" using heat or a medium. The permanency of the pigment color on the fabric can be affected by many things including:

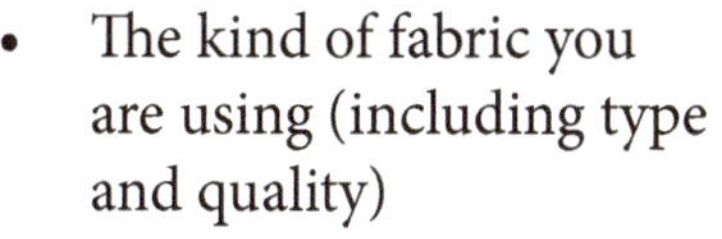

- The kind of pigment you are using (including type and quality)
- The kind of fabric you are using (including type and quality)
- The binders that are part of the pigment delivery method (including type and quality)
- How thick the pigment is applied to the fabric
- What fabric medium is being used with the pigments
- How the resulting colored fabric will be used; handling may affect pigment permanency

- What method you use to clean your fabric, should that become necessary

If you know ahead of time what you plan to do with the fabric to finish your project, or how you are going to use the fabric, you may want to make a sample and take it through your planned process to see what may happen. Based on the results, you can make changes to minimize negative effects.

<u>Note</u>: Please be sure to read labels and instructions. If you are using "fabric" paint, you will usually have to set the paint onto the fabric with heat, not so for regular acrylic artists' paints. Some pigments benefit from heat-setting as a final step. Although the recommendation is to heat-set after the paint (or pigment) is dry, I have not seen any difference if I heat-set colored pigments while they are wet (not dry) except that the pressing of the iron and the heat may "push" the pigments outward. Be sure to protect the iron and ironing surface. The amount of pigment used (how thickly it is applied on the fabric) can also affect things.

Many manufacturers have tips and recommendations on their websites. Unless their advice includes using the pigments on fabric, you are in new territory. Experimentation on test fabric is key before committing to using it on your project.

The most common method for heat-setting is using a hot iron. There are other methods, including clothes dryers, an oven on a low setting, a heat gun/hair dryer, or a heat press. In some cases, leaving a design out over time to let it "cure" also works. For the exercises in this book, using a hot iron for setting the pigments is recommended.

### *How to Heat-Set Pigments on Fabric Using a Dry Iron*

For the Learning Activities in this book, the fastest and easiest way to heat-set your pigments is using a hot iron. If you have never ironed fabric to heat-set if before, refer to the instructions below.

1. Use a pre-heated iron - med-high, no steam.

2. Use parchment paper on your ironing surface and have a piece to use as you iron on top of your fabric to protect the iron soleplate (underside).

3. Place a fabric/FP unit on the parchment paper on the ironing surface. How you place it is not important since both sides will be protected using parchment paper. It may be better to have it placed so you can observe the pigments and perhaps gauge the success of the stabilization process.

4. Place another piece of parchment paper on top of the fabric/FP unit.

5. Place the hot iron on top of the stack and hold there for 15 to 20 seconds. Move the iron to another spot and continue. You want to heat the fabric consistently across its surface.

6. If you want to check the top surface of your piece, lift the parchment paper and look. Carefully replace the parchment paper where it was to minimize potential pigment contamination on other parts of your project.

7. Lift iron and set aside. Turn off the iron as a safety measure. Let things cool before handling the fabric/FP unit.

## CAUTION!

- Do not use steam when using parchment paper. It may cause injury!

- Surfaces will get hot! Don't burn your fingers!

- Wear an overshirt to protect your clothing; Pigment can travel

## Tips!

- You can combine heat-setting your pigments with re-adhering your fabric to the FP for stabilization.

- When you use parchment paper to protect your surfaces, check it to see how much pigment remains behind on it after use; replace with a clean sheet when the parchment paper gets dirty with pigment; otherwise, you may find pigment traveling and potentially staining everything

## Cleaning Up After Using Pigments

If you follow the recommendations outlined above, clean-up should be very straight-forward. Of course, this depends on the kinds of pigments you have been using. The more careful you are when using pigments, the easier clean-up will be.

If your workspace is relatively free of pigments, you may continue using it. Folding your plastic covering materials and taking them outside to shake them, may remove most of the pigment residue. A warm rag can be used to wipe down the surface. Be sure to rinse the rag to remove any pigments.

In some cases, the best option is to discard the covering materials. When doing so, be careful to fold the surface materials into each other, capturing whatever loose pigment has been left behind, and place in a plastic bag or bin. Be aware that pigments can travel during this process, so take precautions.

Always wash your hands with soap and warm water occasionally to minimize cross-contaminating things you touch. Keep a damp cloth at your workspace to wipe your hands on. It will help to keep your hands cleaner and the wet cloth will hold pigment particles better than a dry paper towel or cloth. This does not replace good handwashing.

"embrace
the
wicking"

@rhondadenneypigmentpatchwork

# Tools and Supply List

## Tools and Supply List

The following general supplies and tools are needed to complete the Learning Activities outlined in this book. I did not include any optional materials in the list. In other words, items that you may want to use, but are not necessary. I don't want you to purchase things you may not actually use.

1. Black ultra-fine-tip marker

2. A mechanical pencil (keeps a sharp point) or lead pencil

3. Pen and paper for notes

4. Old cover shirt to protect your clothing

5. Muslin or 100% cotton fabric (light color) (Note: Not all muslins are made of 100% cotton - it is better to use one that is for these activities) - you should have a minimum of two yards of fabric - you will cut the fabric to size as you need it

6. Freezer paper, at least a roll

7. Derwent brand Inktense pencils (a set of at least 24 colors is recommended - if you have a larger set, that is great)

8. A variety of inexpensive paint brushes of various sizes, none very large (you can usually find adequate brushes at a dollar store or, if you already have brushes, you can use them) - you will find out quickly which brushes you like

9. Light box or access to a window for copying patterns to fabric

10. Iron and ironing surface

11. Parchment (baking) paper for iron surface and under iron to protect it from pigments (you will also use this to protect your hands while coloring on the fabric with pigments - refer to Tips and Advice for details)

12. Bottle caps or small containers to hold water and other gels or liquids (this limits the amount of water near your workspace)

13. Water in small containers to pour into bottle caps, as needed (also to rinse off your brushes, as needed) - this limits potentially messy water spills

14. Paper towels

15. Pencil sharpener (preferably a higher quality metal one that has blades that can be tightened and sharpened) and a small, lidded container to catch and hold pencil shavings

16. Plastic or paper to cover and protect tables from pigments

17. Tape to secure fabric when tracing and drawing (blue or green painters tape is best; otherwise, masking tape)

18. Patterns and Reference Materials from this book - these are located in the Resources section at the back of the book

### *Your Assignment - Tools and Supply List*

Your assignment: Using this list of recommended tools and supplies, gather items together or at

least know where you can find them. You will not need everything at once. You are welcome to use any other tools or supplies as well.

## Part 1 - My Approach

### Using this Book

This book is designed to be used by several different audiences interested in learning to use pigments to color on fabric:

- Someone with little or no knowledge or experience with quilting

- Someone experienced with quilting

- Someone experienced with pigments but minimal quilting knowledge or experience

- Someone experienced with pigments and quilting who wants to expand their knowledge

If you have already used pigments to color on fabric, I invite you to set aside what you know and follow the steps outlined in this book. Follow the instructions as closely as you can. Do not jump ahead because you may already be familiar and want to play differently. There is a method to the structure of this book and associated Learning Activities.



Please participate with an open mind; that is the best way to learn a new skill. There are many different ways to use pigments on fabric. My goal is to teach you techniques that have served me well. That doesn't mean there aren't other techniques, or even slight variations of my techniques, that can be used.

The wonder and challenge of the variety of pigments that are available to us, as well as the numerous "fabrics" (or substrates or whatever you want to call them) you see in art quilts, lend themselves to an endless possibility of combinations. That is why I don't know all the answers! Many times my answer to a question that starts with something like "What happens if I . . . " is "I really don't know! I haven't tried that! Try it yourself and let me know."

### Rhonda's 8-week Get Pigment Confident (GPC) Challenge

This book is a study of my techniques. We all learn differently. If you prefer someone to guide you through the topics and Learning Activities in this book, I offer a structured 8-week Get Pigment Confident (GPC) Challenge (with two bonus weeks at the end). You can use this book as a companion to that process.

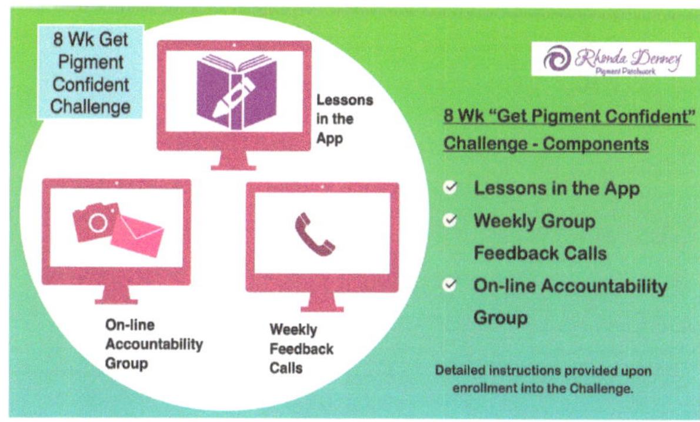


GPC Challenge content is presented in a weekly content drop through a web-based application that you can access any time, anywhere you have internet access, allowing you total flexibility with your time schedule. During the Challenge there is an accountability group to help motivate and challenge you and share pictures of your projects. The small group-learning environment provides the opportunity to connect with others with the same interests in learning and experimenting with coloring on fabric. There is a weekly Zoom call during which participants may ask questions, share and celebrate accomplishments, and get support. At the same time, I can demonstrate techniques, answer questions, and support you.

I offer my GPC Challenges throughout the year and based on demand. Details are on my website, www. RhondaDenney.com. While visiting my website, you can see my portfolio of fiber art, look at my blog entries, and peruse my offerings. You can sign up for my Newsletter. You can also schedule a free call with me to talk about your goals. You can also explore the idea of using my GPC Challenge to augment your use of this book to learn.

### My Goal with this Book

My goal with this book is to offer instructions and insights for coloring fabric using pigments. Whether you have never colored on fabric, have some experience using pigments, or consider yourself very experienced, I hope you will learn something from my tips and advice.

The techniques, tips, and recommendations in this book apply not only to the Learning Activities in the book but can be used as references for any future project for which you want to use pigments. The contents are based on my own lessons learned.

This book contains:

- Basic introductory and some detailed information pertaining to pigments, fabrics, and patchwork techniques

- Information about my techniques

- Advice and recommendations about fabric projects using pigments

- Exercises designed specifically for you to learn my techniques

- Patterns for the Learning Activities that are appropriate to the task

- Tips and suggestions for finishing a quilt top that you used colorant to embellish, hopefully ensuring that your design continues to sing with your creative voice

- Suggestions on where to go next in your Pigment Patchwork journey

- Highlights of some of my own projects, illustrating my Pigment Patchwork techniques and giving you some inspiration

### Why Do I Use Patterns for the Exercises in this Book?

The subject matter for the Learning Activities has been decided for you, using my supplied patterns, unless otherwise specified. I did this for a reason. Using my patterns saves you time so you can concentrate on learning my techniques for testing and using pigments to color on fabric. Whatever your level of knowledge, you will find something to learn here.

If you feel a little intimidated by my patterns, don't give up. I have used these patterns for years in my in-person workshops with great success. Have faith in my process and you may be surprised at what you create. Give yourself a chance and go for it. The results and happy faces of my workshop attendees prove that you can do this!

Even if you don't care for the pattern choices, there are things you will learn by making yourself use them. Remember, the patterns are only a guideline.

By using my patterns, you won't have to worry about determining what you will use as your subject in the exercises. The examples I use in the book are pertinent to those patterns and are identified in the book sections when they are used. The actual patterns are in the back of the

book. Make a copy of the line patterns to use as appropriate.

In addition to a line pattern, I have included reference materials, usually the original color photo used for inspiration, a black-and-white version of the photo and a picture of a sample colored project. If the pattern is one that I created, there will be no inspiration photographs except for my samples. The reference materials are in the back of the book. You can either refer to the reference material in the book, or make a copy to use, your choice.

I do not cover the subject of making your own patterns in this book. That advanced topic will be included in a follow-up book and/or class.

### Words of Inspiration

You do not have to be an "artist" to use pigments to color on fabric. You do not need to have a 

lot of knowledge or background in art to use pigments effectively in your work. It is a skill that can be developed.

My adventures into coloring on fabric started because I could not find flesh-colored fabric for a fiber piece I wanted to create. I found a class that got me started and I learned from there. I realized that I had other options. I could take fabric and add the details to my appliqué pieces or whole cloth using pigments. The stitching would add even more dimension. It opened up a whole new world. Now, because I understand the techniques of adding pigment color to fabric, the possibilities are endless.

Please do not talk yourself out of investing in developing your skills because you lack confidence in yourself. Go ahead. Take the plunge. I believe this book will change how you think about yourself and your abilities. It might take a bit of extra courage to get started but, once you experience what you can do, I don't think you will ever look back!

Plan your journey into the use of pigments on fabric using this book. Have fun! I cannot stress that enough. We learn so much more when we are willing to play and experiment. Join in the fun, explore using pigments to color on fabric. You, too, can be a Pigment Trailblazer!

# Part 2 - Getting Acquainted - Let's Color!

## Part 2 - Getting Aquainted - Lets Color

### Introduction to Derwent Inktense Pencils

I chose to feature one main pigment for the Learning Activities in this book. To help facilitate your learning, I wanted to simplify your choices. I wanted one pigment that was colorful, versatile, and suitable to use on fabric. Derwent Inktense pencils are my pigment of choice.

Derwent is a British company that manufactures pigments of various kinds. I believe it is the only company that manufactures ink-based pencils and blocks. I chose these pigments because they react with moisture and flow, thus you can experiment with them in many ways. I love the interesting results I get when using them.

Derwent pencils:

- Are wax-based, firm, with a highly pigmented core for vivid ink-like color

- Can be used with water to create ink-like washes, but once dry, Inktense is permanent and can be worked over without affecting previous layers

- Have intense, vibrant color which is suitable for use on fabric and other surfaces

For this first Learning Activity, you will be introduced to Derwent Inktense pencils. From this beginning, you will explore more aspects of using this particular pigment on fabric. Enjoy getting acquainted!

### Supplies Needed for this Exercise

A. Flat, non-textured work surface covered with plastic or paper

B. Derwent Inktense pencils

C. Sharpener and shavings container

D. Pencil or mechanical pencil

E. Butterflies pattern from this book, printed onto paper (see section below)

F. White or light-colored fabric (cotton or muslin recommended) see cutting instructions in the instructions to come

G. Freezer paper (see cutting instructions in the instructions to come)

H. Light box or window for natural light, if needed

I. Tape (painters tape recommended, or masking tape)

J.   Parchment paper (cut as needed based on detailed assignment instructions)

K.   Iron and ironing surface

L.   Digital camera or phone camera

## *Pattern for Let's Color! - Butterflies*

The Butterflies pattern for this first activity was inspired by a stained-glass window. Notice the heavy pattern lines to make it look like stained glass. You may choose to create your project using thick lines as in the pattern provided, or to de-emphasize those lines.

The full-sized pattern is in the Pattern Resources section at the back of this book. The supplied pattern has duplicate images of Butterflies on one page. Please make a photocopy of the pattern to use for this Learning Activity.

## *Let's Color! Part 1 - Color on Fabric Alone*

### Part 1 Instructions

If this is your first time coloring on fabric, this entire experience will be new to you. If you have already colored on fabric using pigments, you may be tempted to deviate from the instructions. The exercises in this book are designed to highlight specific processes and techniques. To maximize your learning, please follow the instructions as written.

Before you begin, read through all of the instructions for Part 1 to get a feel for them. Then, gather your supplies and use the step-by-step instructions to guide you through the activity.

Note 1: Fabric Cutting Instructions. You have two options:

- Use a piece of fabric that is the same size as the 8 ½ " x 11" paper that your Butterflies patterns are  printed on. You will use one side of the fabric for this activity, and then you can use the other half of the fabric for Part 2; or

- Use two separate pieces of fabric, each approximately 5 ½" x 8 ½". Use one for Part 1, and the other piece for Part 2.

Note 2:  The Butterflies pattern has very dark lines on it. You may not need to use a light box or window to see the lines to transfer the pattern onto your fabric. These instructions, including the photos, do not use a light aid. If you want to use a light box or window, the process will be similar.

### Part 1, Step 1 Assignment: Transfer one of the Butterflies patterns onto the fabric

Unless you have a work surface that is easy to clean, covering your work area with plastic or paper whenever using pigments on fabric is a Pigment Patchwork Best Practice. Make sure this is done before you begin. Hopefully, this will soon become a good habit.

If you are experienced at transferring a pattern onto fabric, go ahead and transfer your pattern, then move on to Part 1, Step 2. If you have never done this before and need more detailed instructions, read on.

A.   Place the printed Butterflies pattern on a smooth surface. Secure the pattern to the surface with a few strategically placed pieces of tape. 

B.   Place the fabric on top of the pattern. Your cut of fabric should be large enough to cover the pattern lines you want to transfer. In this first Activity,

you need only one set of butterflies to color. You will use the other set of butterflies in Part 2.

C.  Secure the fabric on top of the pattern using tape. This will ensure the fabric doesn't slip in the process of drawing your lines on the fabric. With this small pattern,

you might not feel that it is necessary to tape anything down. However, this is a Pigment Patchwork Best Practice and doing this now will help you continue to use this approach every time you transfer a pattern to fabric.

D.  Trace the pattern onto the fabric.

*   Remember to keep your pattern lines light; the lines should be dark enough for you to see them, but light enough in case you want to hide them by coloring over them

*   Draw only the lines you want to transfer to the fabric

*   Remember, this is your design; the pattern is only a guide; you decide what lines to transfer

E.  You can see the pattern transfer lines on my fabric in this sample. it is laid on top of my cutting mat surface.

**Part 1, Step 2 Assignment: Color the Butterflies using your Inktense pencils**

With your pattern lines transferred to your fabric, you are ready to color. During this step, watch what happens and take notes. Open your

senses and be truly aware of the interaction of the pigments on the fabric.

A.  Place your fabric with the traced pattern on a flat surface.

B.  Experiment using the pencils on the fabric. Observe what happens. Color. If you are nervous, think about how you used to color as a child; this is no different. Suggestions:

*   Color back and forth, round and round, all in one direction; anyway you want

*   Play with shading and mixing colors together

*   There are no rules here except to use Inktense pigments dry (like a colored pencil)

*   Give yourself permission to play; have fun!

*   These are your butterflies; color them any color you like, or a combination of colors

*   Feel free to color everything, the butterflies and the background

*   Experiment creating lighter and darker areas in your design

C.  Document the progress of your project using the camera on your phone or digital camera

When you are done coloring, go on to Part 1, Lessons Learned.

**Part 1, Lessons Learned**

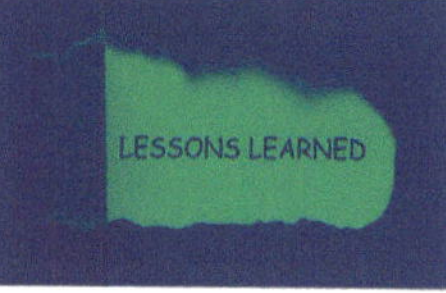


Think back and examine what happened, how you felt, and what you experienced during this activity.

1.  Was it fun?

2.  Was it frustrating? Why?

3.  Could you intensify your colors? Did you use different pressures when coloring?

What results did you see doing that? Did you use layers of pigment to darken or blend things?

4. Did you discover textures coming through as you colored? If so, can you figure out why?

5. Did you have to stabilize the fabric to color on it? How did you do that? Did you use tape or your fingers?

Regardless of what you did, there were lots of learning opportunities from doing this exercise. This is generally how we learn . . . doing and reflecting, changing, and improving the way we do things. This will not be an exception, as you will see in the next activity.

Here are some examples of colored butterflies as inspiration.

## *Let's Color! Part 2 - Color on Stabilized Fabric*

### Part 2 Instructions

Before you begin, read through all of the instructions for Part 1 to get a feel for them. Then, gather your supplies and use the step-by-step instructions to guide you through the activity.

<u>Note</u>: Freezer paper (FP) cutting Instructions. Regardless of the size of fabric you cut for this Learning Activity, cut a piece of FP that is 5 ½" x 8 ½".

### Part 2, Step 1 Assignment: Iron fabric onto freezer paper (FP).

You want to stabilize your fabric coloring surface for this part of the Learning Activity, using one 5 ½" x 8 ½" piece of FP:

- If you are using an 8 ½" x 11" piece of fabric, iron one 5 ½" x 8 ½" FP piece to the back of the unused side (uncolored side) of the fabric

- If you are using the two 5 ½" x 8 ½" pieces of fabric, iron one 5 ½" x 8 ½" FP piece to the back of the unused (uncolored) 5 ½" x 8 ½" fabric

If you don't know how to do this, please refer to Tips and Advice, How to Iron your Fabric onto Freezer Paper (FP) for detailed instructions.

### Part 2, Step 2 Assignment: Transfer second Butterflies pattern to fabric.

As you did for Part 1, transfer the lines from the Butterflies pattern onto your fabric/freezer paper unit. For tips on how to do this, refer back to Part 1, Step 1 above.

### Part 2, Step 3 Assignment: Coloring the second set of Butterflies using Inktense pencils

This is basically the same assignment that you did in Part 1, Step 2. Color your butterflies.

Refer back to that section for ideas on what to do. The goal of this exercise is for you to experience what it is like to color on fabric that has been stabilized. Observe what happens. Take notes and photographs to help you remember. When you are done coloring, go on to Part 2, Lessons Learned.

### Part 2, Lessons Learned

Let's examine what happened. What did you experience during this activity? Was it any different? If so, what differences did you experience? Hopefully you will see (and experience) the advantages to stabilizing your fabric for coloring using pigments.

In the next part of this Learning Activity, you will practice one of the ways to help stabilize your pigments on the fabric.

## *Let's Color! Part 3 - Fixing Pigments on Fabric Using Dry Heat*

### Part 3 Instructions

In Tips and Advice, Pigment Permanency on Fabric, you learned about the permanency of pigments on fabric and were introduced to various methods that can support that. Step-by-step instructions for this method are outlined in How to Heat-set Pigments on Fabric using a Dry Iron. You will practice this method using the Butterflies colorings you created in Part 1 and Part 2 of this Learning Activity.

There are a few things to consider with this method of stabilizing your pigments on your fabric/FP unit:

- The heat may affect the consistency and behavior of the pigments; you will soon learn more about what this means

- Results of this method are not guaranteed; that is the nature of coloring on fabric; the recommendation is to repeat this process often while coloring

- Pressing with dry heat also helps resecure your fabric to the FP

### Part 3, Step 1 Assignment: Review the Process

Review the directions in Tips and Advice, How to Heat-set Pigments on Fabric using a Dry Iron. Gather the required materials and equipment together.

### Part 3, Step 2 Assignment: Stabilize the Pigments on Fabric using a Hot Iron

Using a hot iron and a protected ironing surface, follow the step-by-step instructions for using dry heat to stabilize the pigments you used on the Butterflies designs you created on fabric.

### Part 3, Observations and Summary

The purpose of this part of the Learning Activity was to give you experience using a hot iron to stabilize pigments on fabric, in case you had never done it before. There are other methods of stabilizing pigments as well. Refer to Tips and Advice, Pigment Permanency on Fabric. You will be using the hot iron method of pigment stabilization for the Learning Activities in this book. Now you are more familiar with the process.

You may have to decide if and when you stabilize your pigments on the fabric during your design process. You will learn later what impacts the use of stabilization methods may have on your design so you will understand this better.

## *Summary - Getting Acquainted - Let's Color!*

Coloring on fabric is much easier if the fabric is stabilized in some way. That was the purpose of having you color on unstabilized fabric first.

Derwent advertises that its Inktense pigments become permanent after they become wet and then dry. We did not use any moisture during this assignment, but you will experience that soon. I wanted to get you started coloring using dry pigment first. That allowed you to focus and learn about some best practices for applying colors to the fabric. That includes using layers of color and blending. You will explore all of this further in later Learning Activities.

If this was the first time you used pigments to color on fabric, welcome to the adventures to come! If you are already experienced, I hope you had fun doing this assignment as well. I get a lot of comments about this activity. Some equate it to being taken back to their earlier years when they had fun coloring. I, too, find that, when I am coloring on fabric using pigments, I tend to relax and lose myself in the process. It can become a comfortable escape from other things in  our lives.

Now that you know what it is like to color on fabric, let's look at pigments and fabric in more detail.

# Part 3 - Essential Elements - Pigments & Fabric

### Why Essential?

Before we start to play and experiment with pigments on fabric, I want to review some of the basics of both pigments and fabric. The discussion on pigments includes high-level concepts of what pigments are, how they are manufactured, and the various packaging options that are available for purchase. The discussion on fabrics includes the basics, high-level concepts of the composition of various types of fabrics, and the fabric manufacturing process.

With that foundation, my hope is that you better understand how different pigments may react to different fibers. Thus, you may be able to anticipate and react to what happens with your own work or, at least, appreciate the importance of experimenting when there are many variables at play.

If any of this information intrigues you, do your own research and dig deeper. The more you understand, the better you will be at analyzing things that happen.

### What is Pigment?

Wikipedia defines pigment as:

> a colored material that is completely or nearly insoluble in water. In contrast, dyes are typically soluble, at least at some stage in their use. Generally, dyes are often organic compounds whereas pigments are often inorganic compounds.

The on-line Merriam-Webster Dictionary defines pigment as:

> a substance that imparts black or white or a color to other materials; esp: a powdered substance that is mixed with a liquid in which it is relatively insoluble and used especially to impart color to coating materials (such as paints) or to inks, plastics, and rubber . . .

Pigments made from iron oxides have been used as colorants since early humans began painting on cave walls.

In this section, I will talk about:

- <u>Color Theory</u> - how we communicate the use of colors, including color systems, color wheels, color schemes, and color types

- <u>Commercial Manufacturing of Colorants</u> - the four categories of colorants, additives, and the various packaging of pigments that you may use

### Color Theory

Color theories create a logical structure for color and give us a way to communicate the intricacies and nuances of color. Basic categories within color theory include:

- Color systems
- Color wheels
- Color types
- Classic color schemes

## Color Theory Terminology

The following terms are important when discussing color theory:

- <u>Value</u> - The lightness/darkness of a hue (color); also called brightness (e.g., light, medium, deep/dark)

- <u>Hue</u> - The specific color, independent of saturation or brightness

- <u>Chroma</u> - The purity of a hue or color; also known as the clarity or saturation or intensity of a color (e.g., soft/muted, medium, clear/bright)

- <u>Saturation</u> - The strength/weakness of a hue; refers to how vibrant, or how gray, a color is

- <u>Shade</u> - Color that is generated by adding black to darken a hue (color)

- <u>Tint</u> - Color that is generated by adding white to lighten or brighten a hue (color)

- <u>Tone</u> - Color that is generated by adding gray (white and black) to make a hue (color) duller

- <u>Greyscale</u> - value with the absence of hue

- <u>Gradation</u> - a subtle change from one aspect of color to another; this can include hue, saturation, value, and opacity

Each term helps to clarify aspects of color and aids in communicating about them.

## A Visual Representation of Hues, Chroma and Value

Albert Munsell introduced his color system (called the Munsell color system) in 1905. This system is a way to measure and identify colors within a three-dimensional space based on hue (the color), value (lightness), and chroma (color saturation).

The Munsell color system is a wonderful, graphic way to understand the relationship between the terms listed earlier. The system has been improved significantly over the years, based on the results of experiments in how humans perceive color. The Munsell system is still in use today.

On the following diagram:

- Value is illustrated by a circle symbol

- Hue is illustrated by a thermometer symbol

- Chroma is illustrated by a sun symbol

Note: The sRGB approximations of the 1943 Munsell color notations, which includes every real color swatch, but the colors have been normalized to fit the sRGB range. – Photo courtesy Datumizer Chart (CC BY-SA 3.0)

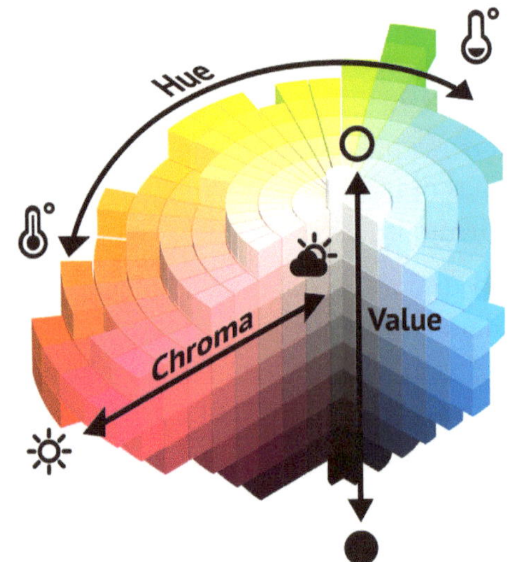


## Color Systems

A color system is a set of colors representing a specific visual spectrum. Each color system is named using the first letters of the colors that make up primaries of that system. There are several different color systems recognized, but I will focus on only three of them.

### RBY Artist color system

RBY stands for red, blue, and yellow. Many of us were taught in school that the three primary colors of the color wheel are red, blue, and yellow (RBY). That color theory

has since been proven outdated, though these three colors are still seen on most color wheels that are used by artists and quilters. Thus, this color system is commonly referred to as the Artist Primaries (RBY).

### CMYK - Subtractive color system

CMYK stands for cyan, magenta, yellow, and key (black). The CMYK color system is referred to as the four-color process because it uses four different colors to produce different hues. The black color is used because the other three colors combined cannot produce a fully-saturated black.

Today, cyan, magenta and yellow (CMY) are the true primary colors in art. Technically CMY are subtractive primaries used in printing inks (mixing paints, dyes, filters, etc.) because, with those three colors (and black), any color can be mixed.

### RGB - Additive color system

RGB stands for red, green, and blue. These colors are the additive primaries, the ones you blend to make other colors when you are mixing light sources such as theatrical lighting, or on a computer or television screen.

This system is best for electronic-based displays, including websites and televisions, because it is an emitted/projected display. Red, green, and blue are combined and added to a black background, thus allowing light to come in. In RGB, the light source comes from behind the color and is pushed to the eye.

### What is the difference between RGB and CMYK?

RGB is an additive color model. CMYK is subtractive. RGB uses white as a combination of all primary colors and black as the absence of light. CMYK, on the other hand, uses white as the natural color of the print background and black as a combination of colored inks.

### The Challenge of Different Color Systems

Colors can look completely different across print and on-screen. To help communicate color effectively,  there are four main color systems in the massive world of print and on-screen design:

- CMYK (for print design)
- RGB (for web and screen design)
- Pantone Matching System (PMS) (a standardized system for print color accuracy or calibration)
- RAL (for powder coatings for physical products and plastics)

Each of these color systems has its own unique applications. Proper use of them will give consistency for a design that goes across printed materials, digital experiences, and even production services (coatings and plastics). For Pigment Patchwork we only need to look at the CMYK and RGB color systems.

## Color Wheels

### What is a Color Wheel?

A color wheel depicts how colors relate to each other. It visually shows the relationships between the color types. The wheel, or circle, is an abstract, illustrative tool that shows the organization of color hues and the relationships between them.

The color wheel I am using in this book is a combination of the CMYK and RGB color systems. If we expand these colors, we can illustrate the entire spectrum including the values, hues, chroma, saturation, shade,

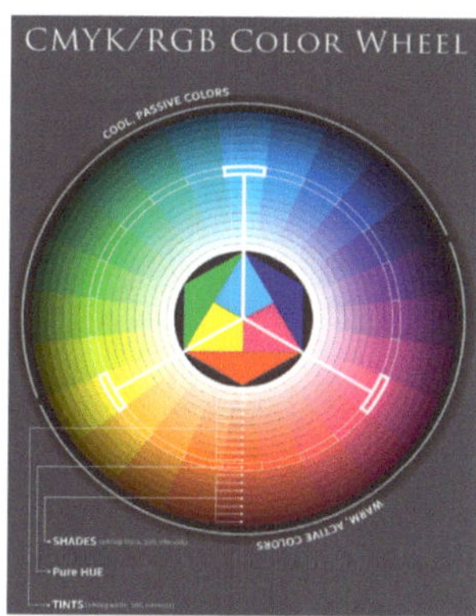

tint, and tone. This is a powerful tool for discussing color or hue and the relationships between them.

## Color Types

There are three different types of colors: primary, secondary, and tertiary colors. Complementary and analogous are considered color types, but they are also considered Classic Color Schemes. For completeness, they will be included in both sections.

### Primary Colors

There are three primary colors: magenta, yellow and cyan (commonly simplified as red, yellow and blue).

### Secondary Colors

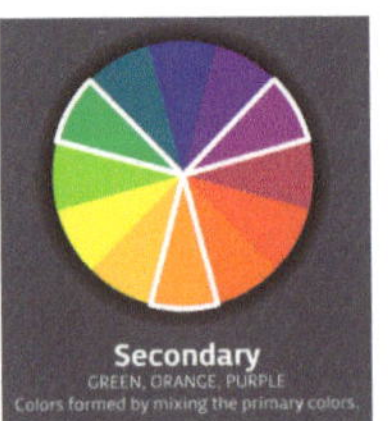

There are three secondary colors: orange, green, and violet. These colors are formed by mixing two primary colors.

### Tertiary Colors

There are six tertiary colors: red-orange, yellow-orange, yellow-green, blue-green, blue-violet, and red-violet. These colors are formed by mixing a primary color with a secondary color.

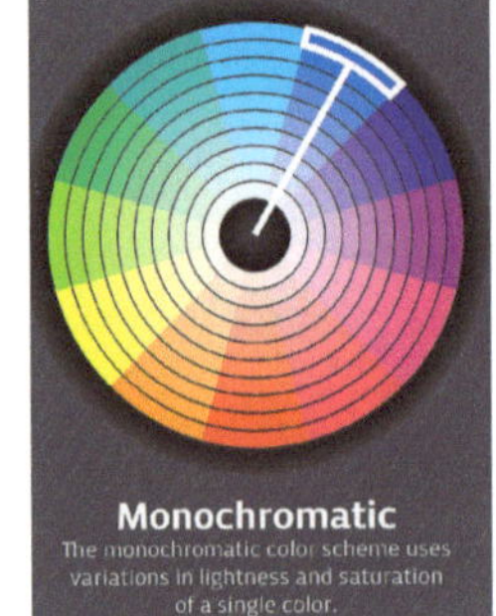

### Complementary Colors

The complementary color type represents a relationship between hues on the color wheel. These are colors that are opposite each other on the color-wheel structure. Complementary colors are also considered a color scheme or palette, so you will see it listed in that section as well.

### Analogous Colors

As a color type, analogous colors are next to each other on the color wheel. Analogous colors are also considered a color scheme or palette, so you will see it listed in that section as well.

## Classic Color Schemes

What is a color scheme? It is a set of colors that work well together to create a unified aesthetic. You may already be familiar with color schemes, especially if you have done much design in quilting. Color schemes are also referred to as color palettes. Let's look at them in more detail.

### Monochromatic

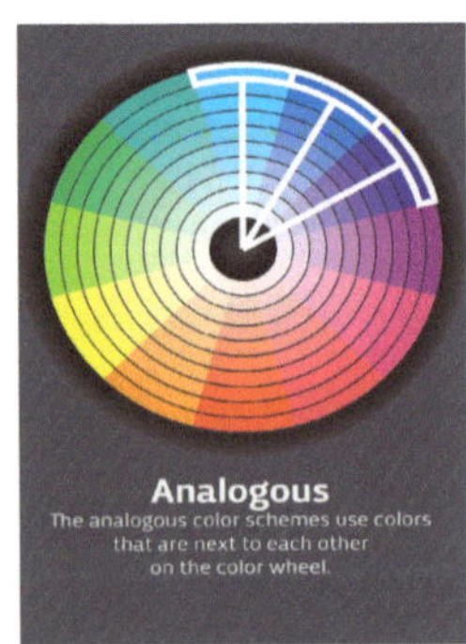

Monochromatic colors are all the tints, tones, and shades of a single hue. These are the colors (the range of values) within a singular section of the color wheel. It can be a range of grays or one color with all its values.

### Analogous

Analogous colors are adjacent to each other on the color wheel. You select one color and its next-door neighbors on the color wheel. You can affect the mood of the design by choosing the run of colors you use.

An analogous run of warm colors is a livelier and more energetic piece. Using an analogous run of cool colors reads as more soothing and serene.

### Complementary

Complementary colors are pairs of colors that are directly opposite each other on the color wheel. When placed next to each other, complementary colors make each other appear brighter. This scheme uses two colors directly across from each other on the color wheel. The colors play off each other. For example, blue and orange. Complementary colors are also considered a Color Type, so it is listed in that section as well. This may cause some confusion.

### Split-Complementary

The split-complementary color scheme is a variation of the complementary color scheme. It includes a main color and the two colors on each side of its complementary (opposite) color on the color wheel. You start with the choice of one color and, instead of using its complementary color, you use the complement's next-door neighbors.

### Double-Complementary

The double-complementary color scheme is also called a rectangle or tetradic color scheme. It can also be referred to as complementary-pairs. It uses four colors arranged in two complementary pairs. If the complementary colors are equally spaced around the wheel, with two colors between the pairs, it can be called an equal tetrad.

### Triadic

The triadic color scheme uses colors that are evenly spaced

around the color wheel. This is also called an equal triad.

### Neutrals

This color scheme uses colors that are unsaturated (or, at least, they should have very little saturation). Your eye will flow from one point to the next in a neutral-flavored space without the distraction of a singular color. Neutrals are visually restful.

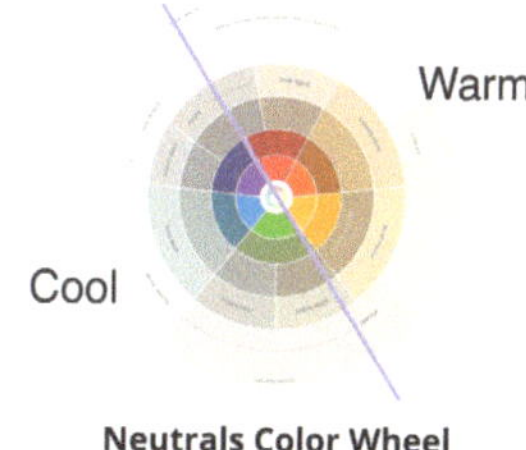



## How to Use Color Theory with Pigment Patchwork Techniques

Analyzing color palettes provides more ways to think about your projects. The terms also help communicate options for the use of various color sets in our work. You are exploring your own creative voice, your song. You may find that you like various combinations more than others.

Don't forget that you can create your color palette using a combination of pigments and fabrics! A colored fabric as a base, instead of white or a light color, can provide a richer color palette. It may also save hours of work coloring on the fabric. In this book's Learning Activities, you will focus initially on the use of pigments on one piece of fabric. In later activities, you can experiment using combinations of fabric colors and pigments in a design.

### Commercial Manufacturing of Pigments

This section focuses on the manufacturing of pigments (colorants), including definitions related to the composition of pigments and how they are packaged that makes them different from each other. I will also give you suggestions on pigments that you can use to color on fabric.

### Important Concepts and Definitions

Do you require a degree in chemistry to understand the differences between dyes, pigments, paints, and inks? With all the various materials that are manufactured today for the application of colorant to things, it may seem so. There is so much information that it can be confusing. Terminology can be common, with different meanings depending on how the term is used.

There are four distinct categories of colorant: dye, paint, pigment, and ink. All the various colorants that we use in art will fit into one of those categories. The categories are distinct because the chemistry behind their manufacturing is different, usually requiring specializations in chemistry or a related scientific field.

### What is the Difference Between Pigments, Inks, Dyes and Paints?

This is a common question when people start investigating all the various options and forms of colorants. Winsor & Newton, the manufacturers of artists' materials, based out of London, England, provides the following clarification:

> A colourant is a substance that is used to impart colour to matter. Dyes and pigments are the main forms of colourant. The main difference between them is that dyes are soluble and pigments are insoluble and are suspended in a medium or binder. This is due to the difference in particle size of dyes and pigments which affects the way they behave.

Quora.com provides this clarification:

> Ink is a liquid or paste that contains pigments or dyes and is used to color a surface to produce an image, text, or design. Ink is used for drawing or writing with a pen, brush, or quill. Paint is a similar substance but is applied with a brush, roller, or pad. Paint is also made to apply in thicker coats than ink.

Manufacturers are always trying to elevate and highlight their own products above their competition, so pigments that are packaged similarly may be called totally different names, making it confusing for buyers.

To add more confusion, different manufacturers may refer to a similar color (hue) by different names or numbers. Most manufacturers of packaged pigments have color charts that can be very helpful in understanding their colors and blending outcomes. Even with that information, I have found it better to test pigments myself before I use them on my Pigment Patchwork projects.

I like using pigments to color on fabric. That doesn't mean I will not use inks or paints or dyes in my work. In fact, many of my fiber art pieces use a combination of various pigments, inks, paints, and even dyes.

**Pigment**
Not soluble in water, larger particles than Dyes
Must be combined with something to help them "stick" to fabric
Tend to stay on top of the fabric
Work on synthetic as well as natural fibers
Require heat setting

**Ink**
Can be either dye ink or pigment ink
Dye ink is available in more colors & is more vibrant
Pigment ink costs more

**Dye**
Soluble in water, completely dissolving
Soaks the entire fiber
Has special attraction for the fiber

**Paint**
Sits on the surface
Usually made with pigments & a binder
E.g. Paintstiks (pigment w/linseed oil)

## Pigment Binders, Vehicles and Mediums

Pigment (color or colorant) by itself has no fixing power, just like a colored powder. To transport the pigment, we need a binder to hold it together and apply it to the support (e.g., fabric, paper, canvas or whatever you are coloring on). The binder can determine the actual color and texture of the pigments. That binder is also the medium or vehicle. In this book, I will use the terms inter-changeably, but my desire is not to confuse you.

Binders are used to keep the pigment in place after the medium dries or sets. In many cases, binders can affect how the pigment dries, allowing more time to manipulate pigment. It can also determine if pigment can be reactivated (rehydrated) so it can be reworked. How well the binder works to support these actions really depends on the surface you are using. You will learn that using fabric as your surface adds intricacies to the equation. The composition of binders can be very complex. Manufacturers are always competing with their competition to improve and surpass the usability and vibrancy of pigments.

## Categories and Types

In my research, I found at least 10 different types of mediums, but they will be categorized by two different properties, oil-based and water-based emulsions. An emulsion is simply a special type of mixture that is made by combining two liquids that normally don't mix; one liquid contains a dispersion of the other liquid, with suspended particles in the mixture.

> Oil-based emulsion is the insoluble medium that has oil as a main component. These mediums are dissolved by organic solvents such as turpentine and petrol. For example, nail polish remover is an organic solvent. Others include linseed oil, dammar gum, and beeswax.
> Oil-based mediums will create a calm and wet color.

Water-based emulsion is a medium that can be diluted with water. For example, animal glue, gum Arabi, casein, egg, and acrylic emulsions. Water-based medium characteristics give a less wet finish but a clear color.

When making pigments, manufacturers can vary the actual color of pigment by mixing them with the different mediums, allowing the creation of hundreds of different colors depending on that combination. Natural pigment characteristics will also determine whether a color formula is opaque, semi-opaque, or transparent.

## Packaging Options - So Many Choices

You can purchase commercial pigments in various forms, packaging, or application products. A good example is watercolors. The type of pigment is similar (watercolor pigments), but the delivery mechanism could be a dry cake (pan), a thick liquid or paste packaged in a metal tube, a pencil, or stick (block).

With such a diversity in the types of supplies and products, it can seem overwhelming wat times. Which to use? My recommendation is to try a few to see what you like and go from there. Different manufacturing brands can produce different results. As art supplies can be very expensive, you may not want to waste money on a larger selection of pigments until you determine that you like and will use them.

## Pigment Composition - Quality vs. Price - Does it Matter?

You can purchase manufactured pigments in artist-grade and student-grade, usually with a cost befitting each grade. The difference? Essentially, the artist-grade has a higher concentration of finely ground pigment with better lightfastness (or permanence) ratings.

Student-grade colors may contain cheaper pigments, more fillers, and extenders.

When you experiment using different pigments on fabric, it might be nice to include some of the different quality products so you can see the differences in their applications. You may find that student-grade works just fine for your project. Or you may fall in love with artist-grade pigments and how they allow your creative voice to sing. There is a balance between economy and performance. In other words, you get what you pay for.

## What Pigments and Application Products Can I Use on Fabric?

To answer this question, pigments will be categorized by the various mediums or application products. We are coloring on fabric, which is very different from paper or treated canvas.

This is not a complete list, but it should help you understand some of your options to try. This list is limited, for the most part, to pigments that can be loosely categorized as either dry or water-soluble. There are a few oil-based items that are included because of their popularity.

<u>Note</u>: Each brand of pigment application products has its own composition, features and flaws. Because there are so many available, examples of manufacturers and/or brand names will not be included. Do your own research when you are considering purchasing pigments.

## "Dry" Pigments

Because they are not normally water-soluble (although there are always exceptions), the following are categorized as "dry" pigments:

- Pastels (soft pastels and chalk)
- Colored pencils
- Markers (inks)
- Other miscellaneous items

***Pastels (Including Soft Pastels and Chalk)***

Even though soft pastels and chalk have been grouped together into one category, soft

pastels are not chalks. They don't usually contain chalk and are very different in many ways. I have successfully used blackboard or pavement chalk on fabric with some wonderful results, but it takes some special techniques to bind or fix the chalk pigment to the fabric permanently. Oil pastels will be discussed in the Other Miscellaneous Items section.

Pastels are available as:

- Soft - Most of these are artist-grade, delivering colors that are pure, brilliant, and intense. Student-grade pastels are not as rich, but both offer the ability to lay down thick color with great blend-ability. These must be fixed to assist in permanency on fabric. These can come in sticks, blocks, chunks, or pan form.

- Medium and Hard - These are firmer to work with than soft pastels because they contain less pigment and more binder. However, that does not mean they are of lesser quality. They are stronger and can be used to make

crisp lines and fine details. They are more break-resistant and produce less dust.

- Pastel Pencils - These are medium and hard pastels in a pencil form so you can sharpen them to get very fine lines. This delivery form also keeps your hands and fingers cleaner.

### Colored Pencils

Professional or artist-grade supplies are generally higher quality than the student-labeled colored pencils. The difference will be in the richness of the hues of color; professional grade colors are typically more vibrant.

There are two types of colored pencils:

- Oil-based - these would be considered more top-of-the-line; not only do these tend to have more pigment in the formula, but the pencil glides easily, depositing pigment smoothly

- Wax-based - these would be more in line with student-grade; the pigments in these pencils can end up becoming brittle and hard to blend

You can also get color sticks (blocks) and woodless pencils. These are essentially a solid core of pigment. Depending on the brand, these can be fun to use and help when you want to lay down large amounts of pigment. However, in other color sticks, the blended core may include a wax base that can affect how they can be used. There are colored pencils that are water-soluble.

Note: All colored pencils can be used for Pigment Patchwork. Student-grade versions will take more effort to lay down the pigment, but they are good to experiment with until you know what you want to do and whether you want to invest in artist-grade versions.

### Markers (Including Alcohol Inks and Other Inks)

There are two types of markers:

- Water-based - these are more typically student-grade. These markers are less expensive, usually disposable (vs. refillable), and widely available. If you ever used Crayola-brand markers, they are water-based. The pigment does not offer much fade resistance. The pigment can be reactivated with water, creating washes. So, technically, these markers could also be referred to as watercolor markers, but the formulas may be different, so I keep them separate.

- Alcohol-based (sometimes called "permanent markers") - These markers would be more in line with professional-grade. They are more expensive, have more colors, and some are refillable. These markers offer better fade resistance but are not lightfast. They do have an odor. Because the pigments are transparent, colors can be layered.

There is an archival spray varnish that can be used on finished marker artwork on paper, but I am hesitant to try it on fabric since I have no experience with it. When I use markers, I have other ways to set the pigment.

You can also use bottles of ink to mark on fabric with stamp pads, sponges, or ink stylus.

### Other Miscellaneous "Dry" Pigment Items

Included in this category are pigments that don't fit into my other classifications, but are still candidates for Pigment Patchwork:

### Makeup

Face/body makeup is essentially pigment in a liquid, powder, or waxy base. So why not try it on fabric? Examples include eye shadows, eyebrow pencils, eyeliners, lip pencils, blushes, foundation, etc.

I would not necessarily recommend lipsticks or makeup that has a waxy consistency. Those items could work; you just need to test them. The fact is that some makeup items may never dry totally or be successfully set or fixed into the fabric. If you don't care about that, then go ahead and use them.

### Oil-based Paint or Pastel Sticks or Bars (e.g., Sennelier Oil Sticks, Shiva Paintstiks, etc.)

These are oil paints in solid form or pastels, made by blending the oil and pigment with wax and pouring it into molds. You will need a well-ventilated area when you use these. Paintstiks are paint - pigment with linseed oil. The linseed oil eventually evaporates from the fabric, leaving the pigment. They call this "curing."

These oil-based sticks are quite popular with surface designers, but they take a long time to dry and cure (like oil paint). Eventually they form a firm skin and then harden throughout. The use of these types of pigments can affect the hand of your fabric, depending on the amount used. Stitching may also be a challenge, with the needle holes remaining. These might be better to apply after your stitching is completed. Experiment and see if it will be okay for your projects.

Note: I do not recommend the use of oil pastels with my Pigment Patchwork techniques. They are usually made with a

non-drying mineral oil so they never completely dry. There is nothing that I know of to seal regular oil pastels. Use at your own risk.

## Water-Soluble Pigments

The following pigments fit into this category because they are generally water-soluble. Some of these pigments can also be used dry.

- Watercolors
- Ink pencils and sticks (blocks)
- Acrylic paint
- Fabric or textile paints
- Other water-soluble pigments

Because of the absorbency of most fabrics, you will find that "wicking" will occur when using wet pigments. Certain resists and mediums can be used to help control some of the wicking action, but they need to be rinsed out of the fabric and they will probably cause more harm than good.

### *Watercolors*

This category includes gouache. Gouache is more opaque than watercolor, giving a matte finish. Watercolors have a luminous quality because of the transparency. Whatever brand you choose for watercolors, the same classifications apply (professional, artist, and student), with the same pigment quality aspects.

You can find watercolors in either tubes or in pans with small, dried cakes of paint. There are also watercolor pencils, which allow you to create using them dry or wet or a combination of the two.

### *Ink Pencils and Blocks (Derwent Inktense)*

I believe that Derwent is the only manufacturer of

ink pencils. I am including their band name because this pigment is oftentimes referred to as Inktense, not just ink pencils. These pencils are as versatile as watercolor pencils but have a firmer texture. They seem to be able to work like traditional pen-and-ink.

The colors are strong and vibrant. They can be used dry for rich, intense color or washed out with a little water to create a vivid translucent effect. Once dry, Derwent claims that the color is permanent and can be worked over with other pigment mediums. I believe this refers to using Inktense on paper. Most reference documentation that I have found recommends using a medium to wet the Inktense pigments to help with its permanency on fabric, though not using water alone. You will soon learn more about Inktense pigments from the Learning Activities in this book.

Derwent offers Inktense in both pencil and block (stick) form. The stick form is useful when you want to lay down large amounts of color on your coloring surface.

### *Acrylic Paint*

Acrylic paints are a synthetic medium made by suspending color pigment in synthetic polymer emulsified by water. They are water-soluble, very stable, and have good adhesive qualities. They resist oxidation and chemical decomposition and will not yellow over time. As with other pigment mediums, acrylic paints come in both professional- and student-grade. This makes them a great candidate for our purposes.

There are also acrylic paints with heavy body, fluid body, and acrylic gouache (like traditional gouache but it becomes water resistant once

dry). And you can also use spray cans of paint on fabric to create some wonderful effects.

### *Fabric or Textile Paints*

Fabric paint, also known as textile paint, is most commonly made using an acrylic polymer. Much like regular acrylic paint,  the polymer is bonded with a color and then emulsified. This makes the paint durable for common use, multiple washes, and exposure to sunlight.

Textile/fabric paint is different from fabric dye. Fabric dyes bond the pigment molecules directly with the fiber molecules of the fabric, resulting in different dyes' being required based on the fabric type used. Fabric paint only aims to bond to the fabric itself, so you don't have to worry about what fabric type you are working with. The results of each are a totally different look and effect.

Textile/fabric paint can be applied to virtually any fabric type, including synthetics, and can also be used on a variety of other surfaces including leather and wood. There are paints that include glitter and some that are glow-in-the-dark. Alcohol-based textile/fabric paint options do exist, but their finishes are lighter and more porous than the acrylic version.

Textile/fabric paints come in several different forms for different applications:

- Liquid fabric paint, for faster coverage for large areas

- Fabric paint markers, with different tips, provide more control for details

- Fabric paint spray, in bottles or spritzers, providing new options for applying it to fabric

- Dimensional fabric paint, also known as Puff Paint. It dries with a textured or raised appearance

*Other Water-soluble Pigments*

The following pigments almost seem to be oxymorons! Due to their manufacturing, they are affected by the addition of water.

<u>**Water-soluble Graphite Color Pencils**</u>

These pencils can be used to create light, medium, and dark washes using water. Or dip the tip of the pencil in water to create soft, smooth lines. There is even one brand that comes in the form of a liquid pencil to create colorful graphite pencil effects.

<u>**Water-soluble Wax Crayons**</u>

When I first saw these wax crayons, I could not believe my eyes. The packaging said that they were water-soluble. My previous experience was with regular wax crayons. These are quite different from the waxy, paper-covered sticks I was used to seeing. Made of higher-quality materials and special binder ingredients that dissolve in water, they can be used either dry or wet.

<u>**Water-soluble Gel Sticks**</u>

These gel sticks go on wet and can be blended, brushed over with a wet paintbrush, spritzed with water, or dissolved to create watercolor effects. Some brands even come in metallic colors. These are fun to experiment with.

## So, What Pigments Should I Invest In?

That is a good question. Each of us is unique. My goal is to help my students discover which artist medium suits them best. Try using a variety, keeping your eyes open to the possibilities. Not only are you using pigments to discover your own creative voice, your choice in pigment mediums may allow you to create using a method unique to you.

## Where Else Can I Find Pigments?

You don't necessarily have to go to a store to purchase new pigments to use. Here are some other potential options to finding pigments you can use on fabric.

## Pigments You May Already Have

Consider pigments that you may already have at your disposal. You may be surprised at all the different pigments that you have accumulated around your house. Gather them together and take stock.

## Your Bathroom Closets or Drawers

Don't forget old makeup! Your friends may even have some they will donate to your creative process. Blushes, eyeshadows, and other cosmetics all contain pigments. Experiment with those items. You might find a good use for them.

## The Soil Around You

You can also make your own pigments using naturally occurring minerals found in soil all around you. These minerals contain metal oxides, principally iron oxides and manganese oxides. These are the pigments that have been used since prehistoric times. The primary types are ochre, sienna, and umber, but there are many more.

There is a process for taking collected earth and gleaning the oxides from it to mix into your own pigments. Look around you at the different colors you see in dirt or topsoil, especially when you travel. You can see all the various color possibilities! I have collected many different colors including yellows, greens, and purples myself.

## Summary - Basics of Pigment

In this section, we started by looking at color, including Color Theory, how we communicate the use of colors through color systems, color wheels, color schemes, and color types. Then we examined the commercial manufacturing of colorants, including the four categories of colorants, additives, and the various packaging of pigments that you may use. That was a lot of information. As you work with different pigments, these concepts will help you recognize their differences. And, even more importantly, why some pigments work differently than others on fabric.

I only expect you to use the Derwent Inktense pencils to complete the Learning Activities in this book, at least initially. Later, you may want to consider trying different pigments in your projects. In fact, I like using a variety of pigments in my work. I am sure that you have other pigments in your household that you will be able to use and learn more about. You will soon have a collection of those pigments that you really like and use a lot. It is not necessary to invest a lot of money in pigments, unless you want to.

### Basics of Fabric

If you are an experienced quilter, you may already be familiar with the term '"thread count"' and have had experience with how different fabrics can be. With my Pigment Patchwork techniques, fabric adds its own unique set of variables to the equation of coloring on fabric.

Let's look at some basics. We need to understand how fabric is made. There are characteristics of fabric and fiber that may add some challenge to your pigment patchwork journey. The information in this section is at a conceptual level. The details might be important in some cases, but an overall understanding is best to start with. You can do your own research if you want to dig deeper.

In this section, I will talk about:

- The structure of fabric
- Types of fabrics
- How fabric can affect the use of pigments

### Structure of Fabric

This includes a basic definition and some of the different types of fibers from which fabric can be made.

### Fiber, Fabric, and Textiles

What is fabric? One on-line dictionary definition is:  **"cloth produced by weaving or knitting textile fibers."** That gives us two general categories of cloth, woven and knitted. That does not take into consideration the variety of fibers that can be used to create textile fibers. We will start there.

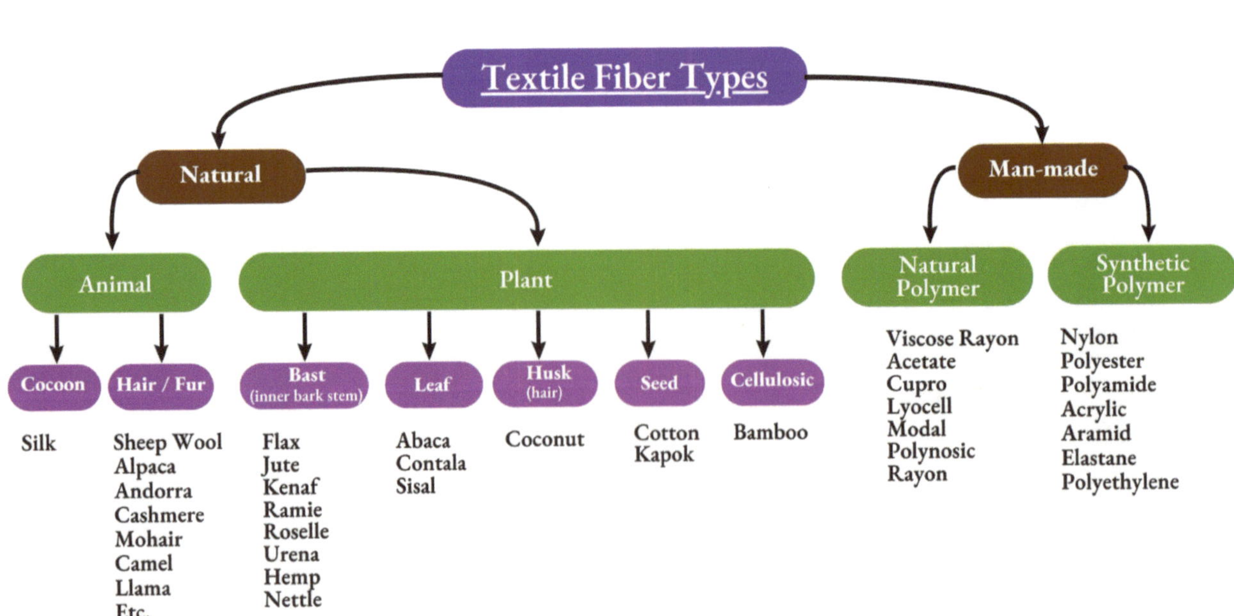

*Types of textile fibers*

The term **fibers** is key. A definition of fibers from the website sewguide.com, defines textile fibers as "**thin threads or filaments**" that are either natural, manufactured, or a combination. The textile fibers are then spun into yarn and made into fabric. The diagram at the bottom of the previous page illustrates the different types of textile fibers.

There are two general fiber types: natural and man-made. Natural fibers can be further broken down into either animal or plant.

Animal fibers are classified as either cocoon fibers such as silk or hair/fur. Things like sheep wool, alpaca fleece, andorra 2-ply blend, cashmere hair, mohair wool, camel hair wool, llama fiber, and other types of hair and fur fit into this latter category.

Plant fibers are categorized by the origin of the fibers, with sub-categories including bast, leaf, husk, seed, and cellulosic. Let's look at some specifics:

- Bast fibers are obtained from the outer cell layers of the stems of various plants; examples include flax, jute, kenaf, ramie, roselle, urena, hemp, and nettle

- Leaf fibers are found in the vascular bundles of plant leaves; examples include abaca (Manila hemp), contala (Agave Contala), and sisal (Agave Sisalana)

- Husk fibers are obtained from the fibrous husks of plant fruits; the main example is coconut, also called coir

- Seed fibers are obtained from the seed hair of plants; examples include cotton and kapok

- Cellulosic fibers are derived from the cellulose found in wood pulp and other woody plants such as bamboo

Man-made fibers can be put into two categories, natural polymer and synthetic polymer. Natural polymers are polymers that are found naturally in our environment. Synthetic polymers are polymers that are produced artificially by humans in a lab.

Examples of textile fibers under the natural polymer category include:

- Viscose rayon (derived from cellulose, the main constituent of plant cell walls; it often looks like silk and feels like cotton)

- Acetate (triacetate cellulose)

- Cupro (a '"regenerated cellulose"' fabric made from cotton waste)

- Lyocell (wood cellulose)

- Modal (a popular cotton alternative made from spinning reconstituted beech tree cellulose)

- Polynosic (a type of microfiber that is a blend of polyester and rayon fibers, with a soft, silky finish)

- Rayon (made from regenerated cellulose, generally derived from wood pulp; usually eucalyptus trees, but any plant can be used; also called artificial silk)

It is amazing what natural -polymer fibers are being made from, and the resulting textiles.

In the synthetic polymer category, most of the textile fibers are forms of plastic created from petroleum- or coal-derived polymers or from naturally occurring materials by chemical modification. Examples include:

- Nylon - an example of a polyamide polymer, produced through condensation polymerization

- Polyester - one of two groups of synthetic fibers with high strength, not easily stretched; there are 3 types: Ethylene (PET), plant-based, and

PCDT (a polyester variant with a different chemical structure)

- Polyamide - another group of synthetic fibers with high strength, not easily stretched and used as textile

- Acrylic - also known as Orion and Acrilan; they closely resemble wool

- Aramid - fibers formed by the poly-condensation polymerization reaction of aromatic diamines and aromatic diacid chlorides; aramids are strong synthetic fibers characterized by excellent resistance to heat, chemicals, and abrasion; Kevlar is an example

- Elastane - a lightweight, synthetic fiber used to make stretchable clothing such as sportswear

- Polyethylene - a popular choice for outdoor furniture fabric and geotextiles, like waterproof paper; a manufactured fiber made of polymerized polyethylene units; often a monofilament but also available as continuous-filament yarns and as staple fiber

Why is understanding the concepts of textile fiber types important to us? The variety of textile fibers used to create fabrics introduces different variables that come into play when we try to embellish the surfaces. Some of these fiber types are not even conducive to coloring on them using pigments. We also need to look at how the fibers are used to create the textiles themselves. This process adds another layer of complexity.

### Fabric Manufacturing

The manufacturing of fabric is a very complex,

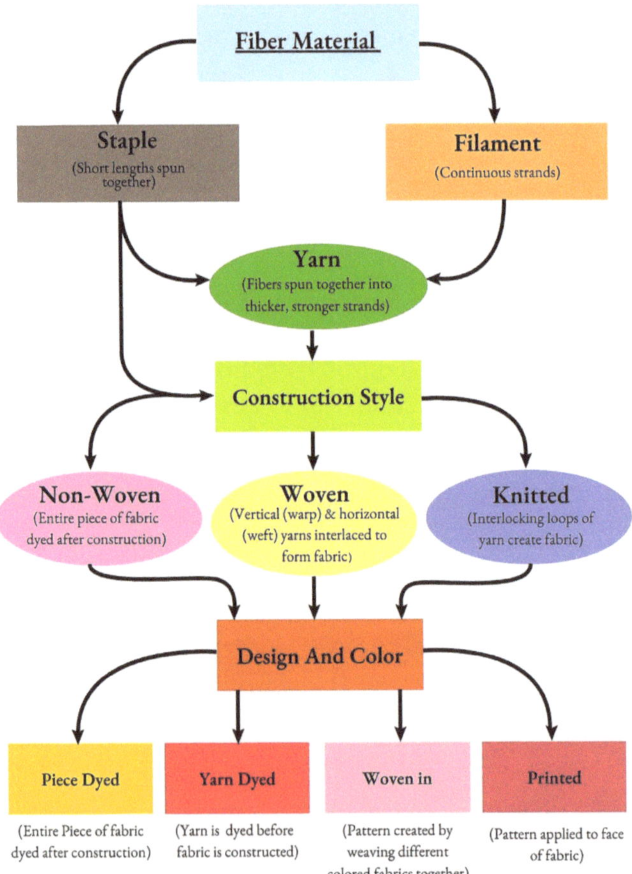

detailed process. One can easily get mired in the minutiae. There are three general steps in the fabric manufacturing process, illustrated in the following diagram:

- Select a fiber to create a material
- Choose a construction style
- Design and color the fabric

### FABRIC MANUFACTURING



Fabric is a material made by entwining fibers. There are two types of fabric based on the fibers used, natural or man-made. Generally, a fabric is named after the fiber used to manufacture it.

Different fibers can be blended, so the resulting fabric is named depending on the fibers used,

the pattern and texture, and the production process used.

Fiber is used to create yarn. Fiber is classified as either staple (short lengths no more than a few inches long) or filament (continuous strands of an indefinite length). Short staple fibers must be spun or twisted together to make a long continuous strand of yarn, sometimes using

filament fiber as an inner core.

Filament fibers (also called continuous filament) have indefinite or extreme lengths and are twisted together to form yarns.

Using yarns, fabric is created either by a weaving or knitting process. Staple fibers can also be used in their original form to produce non-woven or felted fabrics. Depending on the desired design and color, fabrics are then processed to create the final fabric. Most commercial fabrics sold today are manufactured using a printed process, giving you a different front and back.

## Types of Fabrics - Why Should I Care?

From the perspective of embellishing, the differences in fabrics are not as important as they would be if we were trying to dye the fibers. We are applying colorant to the surface. The resulting artwork will not usually be subjected to washing. However, there are aspects of fabric that can affect even what we are trying to do.

That is why my approach has always included experimentation with coloring, using trial and

error. The techniques explored in this book can be used on many different fabrics. The outcomes may be very different. With a basic understanding of the fabric manufacturing process, your analysis of the results will be improved. You may be able to predict what coloring on a type of fabric will produce and challenges that may result. Better yet, keeping notes on your experimentation, including photographs and the name of the fabric, will help. Keeping a swatch of the fabric for future identification purposes is also good.

Most of the types of fabric that you will be using in art quilts fall into the category of woven, and that is where the focus will be.

## Woven Fabric – How it can affect the use of Pigments

The structure of woven fabric and other aspects can affect the results of coloring with pigments. Let's look at this in more detail.

## Woven Fabric

In general, woven fabrics are the structural combination of warp and weft yarn. This diagram shows the structure, along with the terminology. The warp and weft yarn combinations can be changed, resulting in different fabric structures. For example: plain, twill, stain, basket, etc. This diagram shows a plain weave.

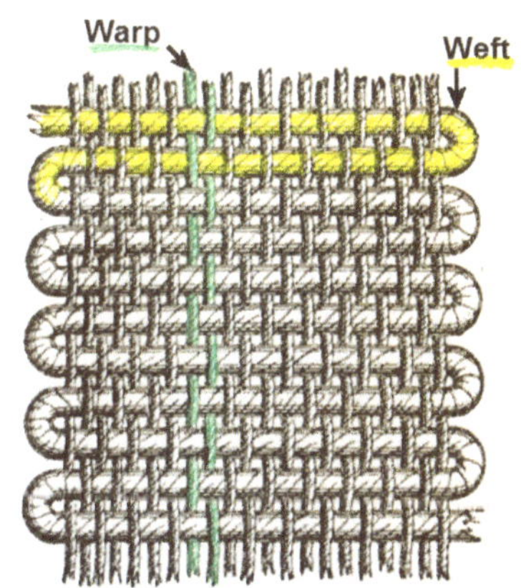
By Alfred Barlow, Ryj, PKM - Adapted from The History and Principles of Weaving by Hand and by Power by , 1878, S. Low, Marston, Searle & Rivington, London., CC BY-SA 3.0, https://commons.wikimedia.org/w/index.php?curid=94725908

You don't need to understand the details of warp and weft as they relate to weaving, or the type of weave system (plain/tabby, twill and satin, or other weaving processes) that are used. However, those aspects can influence how pigments attach to fabric which, in turn, may affect how durable the pigments will be when they are applied to the fabric. You will also clearly see the different textures from the weave systems when you color the fabric using pigments.

The differences between dyed fabric and fabric colored with pigments can be illustrated by examining the top and side structure of the woven fabric.

### Woven Fabric Structure - Dyed Fabric

This dyed fabric diagram shows the result of the dyeing process; conceptually, pigment has permeated the entire fiber structure of the fabric.

### Woven Fabric Structure - Colored Fabric

This diagram shows what happens when pigments are "colored" or applied to the fabric. With a few exceptions (Inktense pencils with liquid added, and some other water-soluble pigments), the pigment laid onto fabric only sits on the surface.

We use techniques and methods to help make the pigments "stick" or get pressed into the fabric for longevity. You can clearly see that fabric coloring is very different from fabric dyeing.

## Other Factors Affecting Embellishment

### Fabric Thread Count

The fibers that make up woven fabric are usually classified by the number of lengthwise (warp) threads and then the widthwise (weft) threads. That is called thread count or threads per inch

(TPI). TPI is an indication of the coarseness or fineness of fabric. Coarser fabrics are more loosely woven,

with a lower thread count; finer fabrics usually have a more dense or higher thread count.

The higher thread count usually indicates a higher quality fabric. Being aware of this in the fabrics you use in your Pigment Patchwork techniques may help explain why the results are not what you expected. Gauge this yourself by testing woven pieces of fabric with different thread counts and see the difference. You may discover that you like what is happening, and it might be exactly what you need for your project.

The cost of fabric is often an indicator of the quality or thread count. Many discount fabrics are more loosely woven. It is not so much how the pigment lays on the fabric as much as what happens when you add moisture to the fabric in the process of coloring.

### Fabric Finishes and Treatments

Another factor that can affect how effectively you can add pigment to fabric is the type of finish or treatment that has been applied during the manufacturing process. Finishes are the processes used on fabric to improve its appearance (and, in some cases, its performance).

Examples of finishes include pre-shrinking, making it non-wrinkle, dyeing to color the fabric, sizing, sanforization, and more. Fabric finishes are applied by dry or wet processes, as well as cold or heated.

Treatments are often combined to achieve a particular look and feel to meet the fabric's functional and aesthetic requirements. A list of 70+ fabric finishes and treatments was found during my research.

We need to think about how the fabric treatment might affect our coloring process, taking steps to either use the finish to our advantage or get rid of any treatments before we color.

## Summary - Basics of Fabric

In this section we examined how fabric and textiles are made, some of the types of fibers and fabrics, and why it is important to you. We looked more closely into woven fabrics and discussed the composition of fabric. We finished by covering thread count and finishes. It is not critical that you understand these topics in detail. You will become more familiar with the concepts as we start using pigments to color on fabric.

You may want to consider trying different fabrics in your projects. In fact, I like using a variety of fabrics in my work. I am confident you already have good candidates in your fabric stash to consider and with which to experiment.

## *Summary - Essentials - Pigments and Fabric*

The pigments you use and the fabric you have as a base will affect the outcome of coloring. This will become apparent to you with the Learning Activity assignments in this book. As a result, your confidence will grow, along with your learning and skills development. Your

observation abilities will increase with practice. You will start to understand why things are happening. With that knowledge, you have a better chance of affecting the outcome when using Pigment Patchwork.

Your Assignment

Derwent Inktense pencils are the primary pigment for the Learning Activities in this book. You will need to purchase them if you do not have access to them. These are a bit of an investment, but I am confident that you will fall in love with them. After completing the first few exercises using the Inktense pencils, you can experiment with other pigments to your heart's desire.

Take a quick inventory of what you already have in terms of pigments and fabric. Make a list of them for subsequent use. The goal of this assignment is to help you acknowledge that you probably already have appropriate pigments and fabrics to play with, except perhaps the Derwent Inktense pencils.

## Part 4: Techniques & Tools: Getting Ready

### Getting Ready to Use Pigments on Your Fabric

#### Check Your Mindset

There are many choices and options when using pigments  in your fiber art. We are all creative in our own way. We all have something that we are good at. Focus on that energy whenever you get discouraged. You can learn to increase your skills through practice and gain more confidence as a result.

Give yourself into the spirit of the exercises and assignments. Play some music to set the mood. Follow instructions, but don't be afraid to try things. Experiment. Recognize the knowledge you gain by giving yourself space to explore. Grant yourself permission to define and expand your own creative voice. To get the most out of this book, I want you to give yourself permission to play. There is no such thing as  a "mistake" in this adventure. Truly, they are all "experiments with an outcome that was not expected"- learn from them.

For the time you spend using this book, I give you a FREE PASS to leave all criticism at the door. Take a deep breath and let the doubts go. Let's tackle this new thing called Pigment Patchwork! There are endless possibilities. Discover what gets you excited about using the pigments. Let it enhance your creative voice. In fact, your Free Pass is good for all  your creative activities, not just when you are using my book. So, take it and run. This process can be so exciting. My hope is that you, too, will become hooked on Pigment Patchwork!

Have you ever watched a young child, dressed  in a cape or a superhero T-shirt, playing superhero? They have no fear. They are ready to take on anything with gusto. Let's do this with the confidence of a 4-year-old in a Batman T-shirt!

#### Decide on Your Project Subject Matter

The first step in any project is to determine your subject matter. That gives you focus for all subsequent activities.

#### For the Learning Activities in This Book

You used my Butterflies pattern for the first  Learning Activity in the book. For the rest of the Learning Assignments, you will use the two line-drawing patterns provided in the Resources section at the back of this  book, Deer Portrait and Koi Fish.  You decide which pattern to use first. The other pattern will be a follow-up project. Make a copy of the line drawing patterns to make them easier to use.

#### For Your Projects in General

Decide on the subject matter for your project. It could be an original design, or something inspired by a photograph or other works. You can then make decisions based on that choice. You can change it at any time, but you must have some place to start.

### *Decisions Before you Start Your Project*

There are more things to consider when you start a project, including:

- Project approach
- Color palette choice
- Fabric selection
- Testing

### Project Approach Choices: Whole Cloth vs. Appliqué

- Whole-cloth design - using a single piece of fabric for the entire design, colored using pigments
- Appliqué design - individual pieces that are cut out from fabric and assembled on a background fabric to make the design

For most of the Learning Activities projects, you will start with a whole-cloth design approach. For other projects, choose the approach to use. This book only covers these two approaches. Regardless of the techniques you use to create a quilt top, you can use pigments to enhance it. Projects using printed fabric panels can also be embellished with color.

### Color Palette Choices

Instructions for each Learning Activity will guide you to choices in color palette for that assignment. For other projects, you will choose the color scheme or color harmony you want to use.

Reference photographs will help you visualize color schemes, even if they are not exactly like your pattern. Artists often use reference photographs for inspiration and as a guide to the details, shading, and color options.

Reference materials in full color are helpful, but it is also good to have a black-and-white version that gives you insights for tones, tints

and shades. That information can be applied to any color palette. The Resources section includes both color and black-and-white reference materials for the two supplied patterns, as well as a sample project image.

To review, color options to consider include:

- Natural or realistic - use the color reference photo to determine the colors you will use
- Monochromatic - using only a range of values within a singular section of the color wheel (all the tints, tones, and shades of a single hue)
- Neutral - colors that are unsaturated or, at least, have very little saturation
- Complementary - pairs of color families that are directly opposite each other on the color wheel
- Equal triad - three-color families that are equally spaced on the color wheel
- Split-complementary triad - a main color and the two colors on each side of its complementary (opposite) color on the color wheel
- Equal tetrad - four complementary colors equally spaced around the color wheel, with two colors between the pairs
- Complementary pairs or rectangular tetrad - four complementary colors close to each other on the color wheel, with just one color between the pairs
- Analogous - colors that are adjacent to each other on the color wheel, using one color and its next-door neighbors on the color wheel

### Fabric Selection and Testing

Instructions in each Learning Activity will identify the fabric(s) you are to use. Initially, your choices are limited

to simplify the process of learning Pigment Patchwork techniques. Samples of the designs shared in the book were created using a similar fabric. Using two different pieces of the fabric, each with a different weight or thread count, will help you understand quality differences in fabrics.

For other projects, decide what fabrics you want to consider and gather them together. Testing both the fabrics and the pigments will help you determine if you made the right choices.

## *Considerations in Using Pigments on Fabric*

The more control you have of all the different variables, the better you will be able to control your results. This includes:

- Preparing your work surface
- Preparing the fabric
- Stabilizing the fabric

Taking steps to help improve the durability and stability of the pigments on the fabric

These considerations apply to the book Learning Activities and your own projects.

### Prepare Your Work Surface

Recommendations for a good workspace are outlined in the Tips and Advice section. Part of that is the surface you will use to color on. Unless you want to introduce texture as part of the coloring process, ensure the surface is smooth. If necessary, use a pad or stack of large paper to cover the surface to make it smooth.

### Preparing Your Fabrics

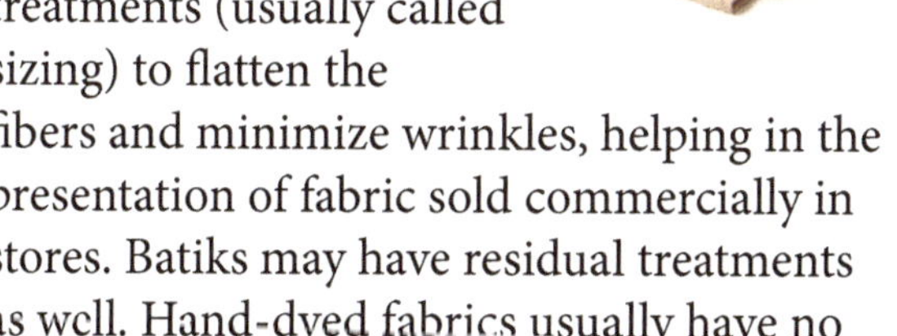

Manufacturers use fabric treatments (usually called sizing) to flatten the fibers and minimize wrinkles, helping in the presentation of fabric sold commercially in stores. Batiks may have residual treatments as well. Hand-dyed fabrics usually have no treatments. Shops sell the fabric as it comes from the manufacturer.

Some quilters pre-wash all their fabrics to remove these treatments, either as they purchase fabric or before they create a quilt. Do we need to wash our fabrics before using Pigment Patchwork techniques on them? My simple answer is "Yes," except for hand-dyed or PFD (Prepared for Dyeing) fabrics.

Why? The treatments on the fabrics may influence how the pigments will take to the fabric. Since most of the pigments we apply will be primarily on the surface of the fabric, it is best to remove anything that may interfere with that process.

If and when you choose to wash the fabric is up to you. You can experiment on the fabric to see if washing is necessary to ensure your pigments will adhere. Then you can make an informed decision.

I usually wash my fabric as I use it, especially if I am using only a small amount at a time. I wash by hand using soap and water and then iron the fabric dry.

### Stabilizing Your Fabrics

You know about methods to stabilize your fabrics before coloring on them. The preferred method is using freezer paper (FP). You will need to prep your fabric before using the FP to stabilize them for your project.

### Planning for Supporting the Permanency of the Pigments

You have already used a hot dry iron to heat-set your Butterflies project. The same concepts apply to all of your projects. Have your iron, ironing station, and parchment paper available.

### Your Assignment

Gather your materials and prepare for next steps. Check to see that you have arranged your workspace appropriately and that you have a smooth coloring surface. You are ready to go.

## *Let's Experiment*

### Create Your Test Sheets

You could simply transfer your pattern to fabric and start coloring, but that is not recommended. Not quite yet. A little proactive experimentation and testing of your pigments on the candidate fabric will uncover potential pitfalls and surprises so they don't negatively affect your project.

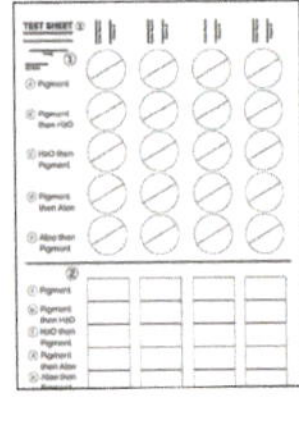

You'll find a generic template for testing pigments in the Resources section at the back of this book. Before you start testing, you should create your own sets of test sheets to use.

Once you use the generic testing template provided, you are welcome to modify the format, tailoring it to your needs, or create a new one.

### Creating your Test Sheets - Supply Needs

You need the following:

- Test-sheet template (two pages), located in the Resources section

- At least two pieces of fabric (the same fabric you chose for your project) cut to fit the template, ironed onto freezer paper (FP) to stabilize it - this makes a fabric/FP set (make a few more sets in case you want to do more testing - you can always make more sets or individual pages as you need them)

- A pencil to create your lines on the fabric/FP sets

### Create and Customize Your Test Sheets

Instructions:

1. Create a fabric/FP set of two for each fabric you want to test. They should be the same size as the generic test-sheet template. These test sheets will fit into a page protector, a notebook, or file folder.

2. There are sections of the test sheet that will be customized:

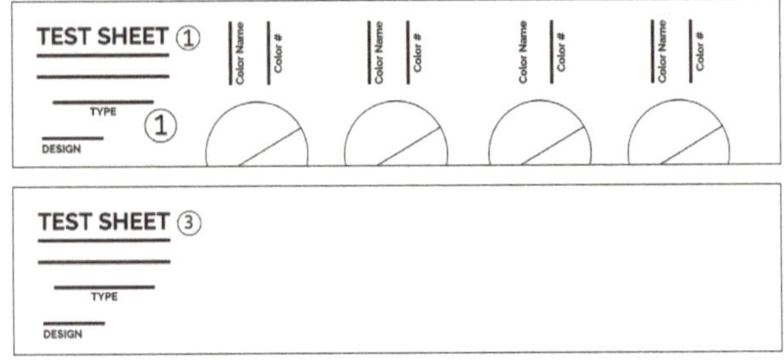


a. The line with the word "Type" under it should be tailored to identify the type of pigment you are testing. Include the brand name as well as the pigment medium or delivery mechanism (e.g., "Inktense pencil" or "Derwent watercolor pencil"). This should be the same for page 1 and 2 of a test-sheet set (fabric/FP). We are using Derwent Inktense pencils for the Learning Activities, so use that label. Optionally, leave this blank and add the label just before using the test sheet.

b. The line with the word "Design" under it should be tailored as appropriate. This label helps link the test sheets to a specific project or pattern. Use words that will help as a reference (e.g., Koi Fish instead of Fish, Deer Portrait instead of Deer, etc.). For other projects, use a title or descriptive words, as appropriate. This label should be on both pages 1 and 2 to help tie them together.

c. There are vertical lines with small labels under them ("Color Name", "Color #") across the top of the template page 1. Those are placeholders for the name of each color being tested (use the manufacturer's name, as well as the manufacturer's color identification number). This is for future reference. Optionally, leave it blank to fill in later.

3. Transfer the test sheet structure to the fabric using a pencil. Using a pen or printing this template onto the fabric is not recommended.

If your fabric/FP sets separate from handling, simply iron to re-secure them before use.

## Your Assignment - Create Your Test Sheets

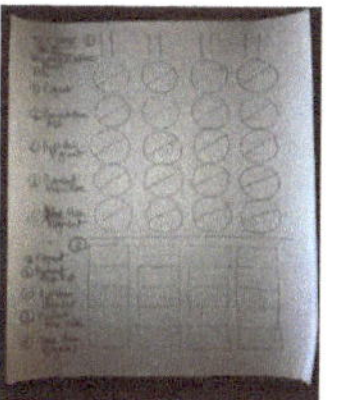

Decide on your fabric to test. For this first Learning Activities project, this will be either cotton or muslin. Create at least one set of test sheets. Remember that the set includes two template sheets (you will have Sections 1, 2 and 3 for each set you make). I recommend creating at least three sets of test sheets so you can play.

### *Example of a Test Sheet*

This is what your test sheets should look like. These were created using a pencil to draw the lines on cotton fabric stabilized on freezer paper.

### *Closeup of Placeholder Spots*

Here are close-up photographs of the top of each sheet. I knew the type of pigment I

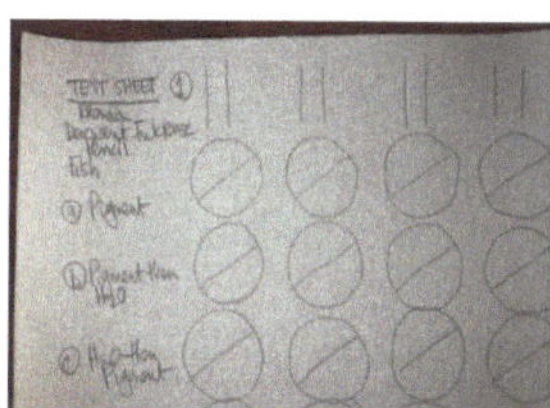

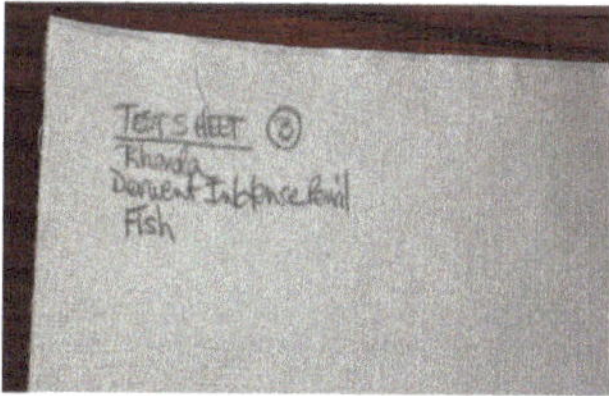

planned to use as well as the design, so I wrote those in. I did not fill in the color names and numbers yet. Lines are used to remind me to fill them in later when I use the test sheet.

## Testing Set Up

Get everything ready to start testing. Gather your pigments, ensure your workspace is set up, your digital camera is handy, and your test sheets are at hand.

## Select pigments

Select the pigments for testing. The colors will be based on the pattern you are using or whatever colors you want to test first. The test sheet with Sections 1 and 2 have room to experiment with four (4) different colors at a time.

### *For the Learning Activities in this Book*

Based on your chosen design pattern (Deer Portrait or Koi Fish) pick out three (3) or four (4) Derwent Inktense pencil colors to test. My recommendations are below. You will choose the actual color you will test with. If you have a larger set of Inktense pencils, you have more choices. (Note: Though not listed, white and black can be used for highlights. Wait to test those colors and their uses until later in Section 3 of the Test Sheet.)

To help you with this, I've included color names from a set of 24 Inktense pencil tin. Please note that your tin may have different colors in it. And, if you have a larger set, you will have other options for color choices. For your initial test, the following are recommended:

Deer Portrait:

- Off-white or light tan (e.g., Antique White, Baked Earth)
- Medium brown (e.g., Willow)
- Medium-dark brown (e.g., Bark)
- Light pink (e.g., Fuchsia)

Koi Fish:

- Yellow (e.g., Sherbet Lemon, Sun Yellow, Mustard)
- Orange (e.g., Tangerine, Baked Earth)
- Light blue (e.g., Iris Blue, Sea Blue)

- Dark blue (e.g.,Deep Indigo, Bright Blue)

Start with these colors. If you have your heart set on a different color palette for your first project, test those colors afterward on different test sheets. This is where your extra test sheets can come in handy. Or create some new test sheets. Later, you will use the results of your testing to decide on the colors you choose for your design.

### Your Projects in General

Decide what colors you want to use in your project. Fill out the test sheets as appropriate. Use the test sheets to experiment with those pigments on the fabrics you plan to use.

## Set-up Your Workspace for Testing

Get your workspace ready. Supplies needed for the testing include:

1. The test sheets you created.
2. The four (4) colors of Derwent Inktense pencils you chose. You might want to have the rest of the box with you. You can also have any other pigments you might want to test.
3. An appropriate workspace.
4. A cover shirt or old clothing you don't mind getting pigment on.
5. Water, paint brushes, gel pen, pencil, sharpener, tape, etc.
6. Parchment paper.
7. Aloe vera gel and water.
8. Small and medium containers to rinse brushes, paper towels, a damp cloth or towel.
9. Your iron and ironing board/surface with parchment paper or similar material.
10. Anything else you want to have handy.

## Why Aloe Vera Gel?

Aloe vera 100% gel will be one of the mediums used in our testing sequence.

Bottle caps can be used to mix colors and hold aloe vera gel. Since aloe can dry out quickly, it is best to start with a small amount and add more aloe as needed. As you use aloe vera gel more, you'll get a better feel for this.

## Update Your Test Sheets

With your pigments selected, update your test sheets appropriately. That includes:

- Your name and the date of testing (handy for later reference)
- The type(s) of pigments being tested, if you left that blank (e.g., Inktense pencils)
- The colors of pigments being tested - the manufacturer's name for the color and the color number

## Plan How You Will Document Your Findings

Think about how you will document your testing results and observations. Things to consider:

- As you are testing, add any comments or observations you have; e.g., you notice immediate wicking, you see some reaction to the test, or you like what happened
- Think ahead of time and plan to take in-progress pictures as you are testing to help you remember what happened; with your camera at the ready, you are more likely to take pictures
- Think about what might be important for you to remember about the testing results and your reactions; notes will help remember the details
- If writing your notes on your fabric, use either a gel pen (less wicking on the fabric) or a soft (dark) lead pencil

## Get Your Camera Ready

Have your digital camera or cell phone out and have it handy to use.

Your photographs and your notes will provide wonderful documentation for use now and in the future.

## *Test Using Section 1 of the Test Sheet*

### Why Are We Doing This?

You want to see the actual color of the pigments you plan to use on the fabric of your choice, and preparing test sheets will provide that information. You may be surprised at how different a color looks on fabric. The base color of your fabric and any mediums you mix with your pigments can influence the resulting color.

Remember to have fun. Each activity of the test sheet sections has a purpose, but there are no strict guidelines. You have the flexibility to discover how best to experiment. You will test through the sections one at a time. Read through the instructions first, then start your testing. Don't forget to write notes.

### How to Use Section 1 of the Test Sheet

You have a choice on how you use this section:

- Color row-by-row, moving across, changing colors for each circle, or

- Pick a color and go column-by-column, moving down (preferred)

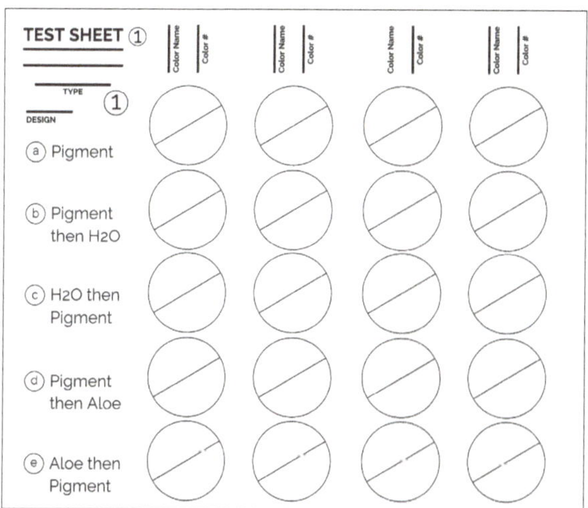


The circles in Section 1 are divided with a line, forming two sections inside. Using your Derwent Inktense pencils, your goal is to create:

- A very light representation of the color in one section (the top one), and

- A very dark representation of the color in the other (lower one)

Try to keep your color inside the lines (there is a reason for doing this).

Each column represents the colors with which you are experimenting. Read all the steps for this section first, then start.

4. <u>Section 1 - Row a - Dry Pigment</u>

   a. This row tests using pigment alone; color the circles as instructed above, with one section light and the other dark.

   b. With this test you are learning how much pressure you need to transfer the pigment to the fabric

   c. Tip: To make your color darker, you may find it better to add layers of pigment instead of pressing down harder with the lead of the pencil

5. <u>Section 1 - Row b - Dry Pigment, Then Water</u>

   a. This row tests adding dry pigment first, then adding water (as a medium) to the pigment

   b. Color the circle sections as directed with the dry pigment, making the top light and the bottom dark

   c. Using a small paintbrush and water, carefully brush the area you colored, blending the color; try to keep the pigment inside the lines

   d. Tips: Be careful to control the amount of water used; blot excess water with a paper towel; brush size can also make a difference; use a smaller brush; notice how the pigment is affected by water.

6.  Section 1 - Row c - Water, Then Pigment

    a.  This row tests using water first, then pigment

    b.  Take a small amount of water on your brush and wet the circle with water

    c.  Using your Inktense pencil, add color to the area; keep the pigment inside the lines; keep one section light and the other dark

    d.  Tips: Keep the amount of water you add to the fabric at a minimum; be very careful adding the pigment to the lighter shade area; you will see how quickly the pigment travels.

7.  Section 1 - Row d - Dry Pigment, Then Aloe

    a.  This row tests what happens with the pigment when you add a different kind of liquid medium, aloe vera gel

    b.  Color the circle sections with the dry pigment first

    c.  Squeeze out a small amount of aloe vera gel into your bottle lid or small container

    d.  Using a small paintbrush, carefully paint aloe onto the surface where you added the pigment; keep the color inside the lines; keep one section light and the other dark

    e.  Tips: It is better to use less aloe than more; use a paper towel to dab some of the extra aloe off the brush before you apply it; the brush size can also make a difference; try a smaller brush; you will see how the pigment reacts with the aloe; take notes on what happens

8.  Section 1 - Row e - Aloe, Then Pigment

    a.  This row tests adding aloe first, then pigment.

    b.  Take a small amount of aloe vera gel on your brush and wet the circle with it; try to wet the fabric thoroughly with the aloe

    c.  Using your pigment, add color to the circle sections; keep the pigment inside the lines; keep one section light and the other dark

    d.  Tips: Don't use too much aloe; to prevent the aloe from drying out on the fabric, consider applying the aloe to one half of the circle at a time

## Your Turn - Now You Do Test Sheet, Section 1

It's your turn. Review the instructions as needed and begin your testing for Test Sheet Section 1. Don't forget to write notes and take pictures. When you are done with your testing in Section 1, continue reading. There will be an example photograph of the section results and some information about what you may have experienced. Use those to compare with your own results. Whatever the results, there are lessons you can learn.

## Observations and Results - Section 1 of the Test Sheet

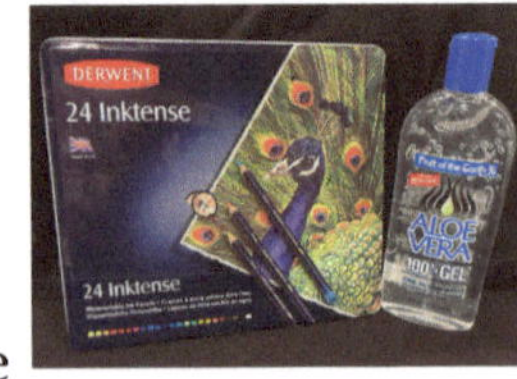

Now that you have done your testing of this section, let's discuss some of the things you may have encountered. Please note that the observations in this section pertain to Derwent Inktense pencils. If you are testing other pigments, your results will be different.

Here is an example of a completed Section 1 Test Sheet. Your test sheet may not look exactly like this; in fact, your test sheets may look different each time you test. The important thing to remember is that you will have gained tremendous insights each time you practice using the pigments.

## Oops! Uh-oh! Wow! *#$&!%

Had I been a fly on your wall, watching you work, I might have heard an occasional "Oops!" "Uh-oh!" "Wow!" and, perhaps, even some cursing! Believe me, that is part of the learning process.

I asked that you give yourself permission to experiment and play. The only way you can truly learn is by doing and seeing what happens. Results cannot really be explained and are not necessarily what we expect or even want.



Now you are starting to know what works and what may not. Or at least you are starting to realize that experimenting and testing are critical components to understanding what may happen.

## Be Kind to Yourself

Be kind to yourself. There is no such thing as mistakes here. They are learning experiences. Whatever your results with this exercise, please don't be hard on yourself. Learn from what happens and, if necessary, try again until you figure out how to accomplish your testing goals and what works best for you.

There are so many ways to apply pigment to fabrics. That, combined with the number and variety of pigments and fabrics available, make it very difficult to predict what will happen. It is best to try various things until you figure out what works for you on a particular fabric using a particular pigment. Then, hope that the behavior continues when you try to repeat that process on your project. Sometimes it doesn't, so be flexible.

You can always create another test sheet and repeat the exercises. Each time you will learn more and your confidence will grow. Your chances of remembering the lessons learned are far greater because you experienced them yourself. Remember that "Practice Makes Progress!" It is not "Practice Makes Perfect" because there is no such thing when it comes to pigments on fabric.

## Embrace the Wicking

You can see the wicking that occured with the sample test sheet above. Even as experienced as I am, I still have to deal with it when using various pigments and mediums on fabric.

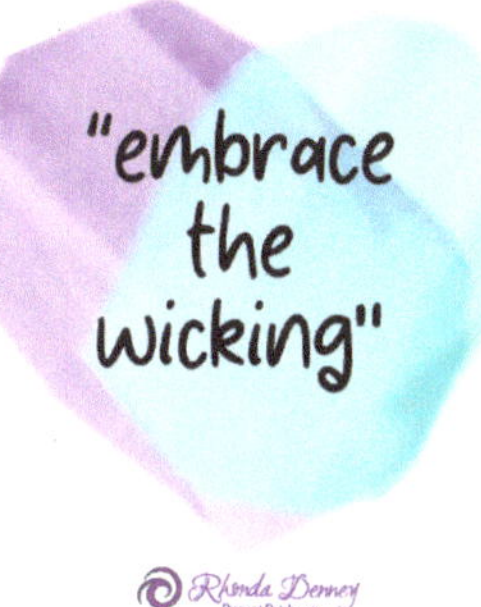


You may have felt frustrated with how difficult it was to keep the pigment inside the lines of your circles on this practice. How better to experience wicking. With the different rows, you were able to see how variable "wicking" can be, and what it does to the fabric. There can be differences in wicking because of a specific pigment or even pigment color formula.

The fabric also plays a hand in this. If you can test different quality fabrics of the same type (a higher and lower thread count), you should clearly see the differences. That additional testing will allow you to make more informed decisions for your project.

How to better control the wicking? With practice, you may learn that carefully adding pigments farther from the edges will help control the movement of the color (i.e.,start in the middle of the section of the circle and move out). Controlling the amount of water or aloe is also key. You probably saw a big difference between the two mediums (water vs. aloe) in terms of wicking action.

The reality is that you cannot totally control what happens, but you can understand it

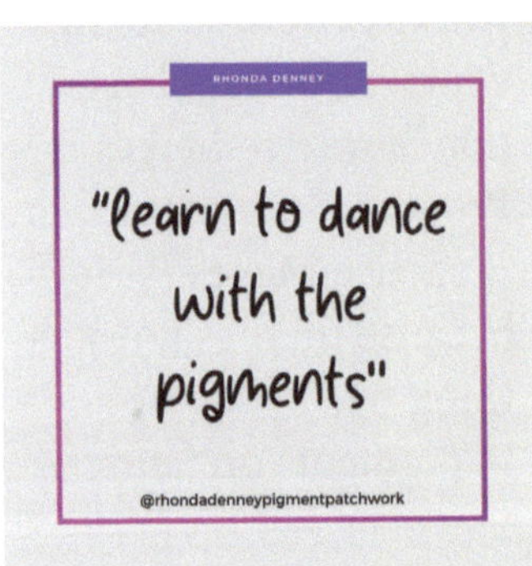


better and work with it, what I call "dancing with the pigments." You can achieve some wonderful results by working with the interaction of the pigment with the fabric. The results may not necessarily have been what you expected, but still a valuable and spontaneous interaction between you, the pigments, and the fabric.

If you are creating a whole-cloth project, controlling the wicking becomes more important. When you are creating smaller pieces that you will cut out to appliqué, wicking may not be such a big issue because you can trim the edges or turn them under. Resulting wicking may force you to change from a

whole-cloth approach to an appliqué approach. We need to be flexible!

Another option is to start over, being more careful with how you add the pigments, learning from your experiences.

### Learning How Much Pigment to Use

Controlling the amount of pigment that you use is very important, but you have to experience it to understand this fully. It is far easier to add pigment than to take it away, especially on fabric. You will have better control if you start light and add more layers of pigment to go darker. Once you have a lot of pigment on the fabric, it is difficult to lighten the color. More on this topic later in the book.

### Learning How and When to Use Other Mediums

Derwent Inktense pencils are soluble and will

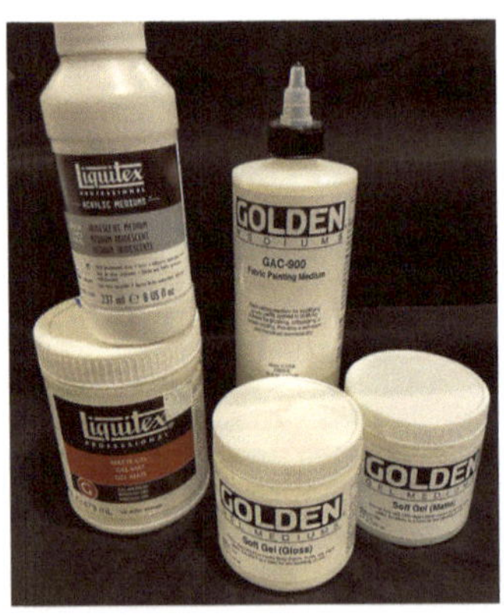

react to moisture, specifically a water medium, which is why they are recommended when learning Pigment Patchwork techniques. Technically, both water and the aloe vera gel are mediums.

There are other mediums as well. You are welcome to try others.

Experience has shown that aloe provides more control over blending and wicking of pigments on fabric. It does not wick as fast, but a lot depends on the amount used. There are times when using only dry pigment is better. Water gives a different effect. With enough experimentation, you can decide what kind of look you want.

It is important to get a feel for working with a medium (in this case, water or aloe) and the pigment. You will find that you can move or push the pigment along using a brush. Careful control of the amount of pigment and medium used, as well as practice using brush techniques, will give you a better chance of manipulating the pigment or controlling where the pigment goes.

## Colors Change When the Fabric Dries

You may love the richness of a pigment when you are using it with a wet medium such as aloe. Realize, however, that a liquid medium will dry, reducing the luster and sheen you see while it is wet. Don't be fooled by the look of "wet" pigments on your fabric. You will have to wait until the fabric dries to see how the color truly looks.

## You Can Always Add Pigment

It is good to know that you can always add more pigment. The handling of the fabric; the bending and folding, cutting, and ironing, beating with the sewing machine needle/foot during machine stitching; or handling during hand-quilting, etc. may cause pigment to detach from the fabric surface. When that happens, you can add more pigment to the surface and "touch up" those areas.

## *More Experimenting - Section 2*

Section 2 allows you to continue exploring with the pigments. You will also continue to develop your own skills coloring on fabric.

Guidelines are the same as in Section 1. Read the instructions through before you start. Refer to the instructions as necessary. While testing, take notes and photographs as appropriate. Don't rely on your memory alone.

## How to Use Section 2 of the Test Sheet

In Section 2 you have a choice as to how you do the testing. You can:

✏ Color row-by-row, changing colors for each rectangle, or

✏ Pick a color and go column-by-column, doing the exercises

②
a Pigment
b Pigment then H2O
c H2O then Pigment
d Pigment then Aloe
e Aloe then Pigment

The rectangles in Section 2 are purposely stacked right on top of each other. The lack of space between the five rectangles in vertical alignment is designed to make your task of controlling wicking a bit more challenging. The columns represent the same four colors you used in Section 1.

Your goal with this section is to create a blending of color starting with a very light representation at one end of the rectangle, moving into a very dark representation at the other end of the rectangle.

In dyeing, this is often referred to as an "ombré," the blending of one color hue to another, usually moving tints and shades from light to dark. Keep your color inside the lines. With your testing experience in Section 1, hopefully Section 2 will be easier for you to do.

9.  <u>Section 2 - Row a - Dry Pigment</u>

    a.  Use pigment to color the rectangle, shading the color from very light to very dark at the other end

    b.  Keep your color inside the lines of the rectangle

    c.  Tip: Try using layers of pigment instead of pressing down hard with the pencil lead

10. <u>Section 2 - Row b - Dry Pigment, Then Water</u>

    a.  Color first with the dry pigment

b.  Then, carefully brush the fabric with water to blend, keeping the color inside the lines

c.  Tips: Blot your brush with a paper towel to remove excess water; try a smaller brush

11. <u>Section 2 - Row c - Water, Then Pigment</u>

a.  Wet the rectangular space of the fabric with water; keep the amount of water to a minimum

b.  Then, use your pigment to add color; keep the pigment inside the lines

c.  Tip: Be very careful adding the pigment to the lighter shade area; pigment may travel quickly!

12. <u>Section 2 - Row d - Dry Pigment, Then Aloe</u>

a.  Color first with the pigment, then add aloe

b.  Create the blending from light to dark, keeping the pigment inside the lines

c.  Tips: Blot your brush with a paper towel to remove excess aloe; try a smaller brush

13. <u>Section 2 - Row e - Aloe, Then Pigment</u>

a.  Wet the fabric inside the rectangles with aloe, then add the pigment, going from light to dark, keeping inside the lines

b.  Tip: Be very careful adding the pigment to the lighter shade area; pigment may travel quickly!

### Your Turn - Section 2

Experiment on your own with your test fabric for Section 2. Go back and review the instructions if you need to. Don't forget to make notes and take pictures. When you are done with the testing for Section 2, read on to see the example of a Section 2 test sheet

and observations about the results of the testing in this section.

### Observations and Results - Section 2

Following is an example of a completed Section 2. Your Section 2 may not look exactly like this. (Hopefully you used the right pigments in the right places, not like me! Oh well, just make a note and move forward!)

As with Section 1, acknowledge that you practiced using the pigment in various ways, and gained tremendous insights by doing so.

Were you able to control the wicking better? This exercise really forces you to think about how you apply the pigments to the fabric to get the depth of the colors you want. Layers seem to work best, as well as using the wet mediums to push the pigments where you hope they will go. When using a wet medium, you may have more control by pushing the colors out to form a lighter blend instead of using pigment. Add pigment judiciously during the process.

Before we go on, I want to point out an interesting learning experience with this example colored Section 2 sheet. If you look closely at the top left of the image above, you can see what I mean. This is a closeup of that area on the same sheet.

This is a clear example of the use of a medium, in this case Aloe, on the fabric affecting how pigment reacts when applied. This was the residual wicking of the

Aloe from the earlier testing of Section 1. When I applied the pigment to this area, you see what happened where this Aloe coated the fabric A good lesson learned! Knowing about it also lets you understand the interaction and could be used to your advantage in a design.

If you still feel that you are not comfortable using the pigments, repeat the exercise. Each time you practice, you should feel more comfortable. Practice Makes Progress! Try using different colors of pigments.

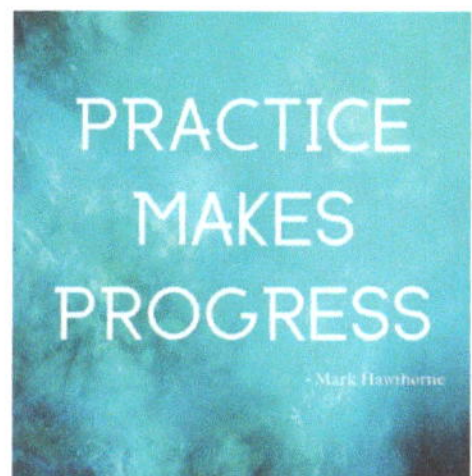

Each time you experiment, you will gain insights into how differently pigments blend and react when coloring.

## *Experiment Specific to Your Project - Section 3*

Section 3 of the test sheet is more project specific. Now that you have a feel for the pigment colors you are considering in your design, we want to start playing or practicing with specific aspects of your project. This section allows you to practice techniques or ideas you might want to consider.

Do your own experimentation. Think about the project. Identify components of the design to practice on, textures or affects you might want to consider.

Remember to have fun and explore. Experiment with textures, shapes, and blending of colors. Feel free to use other pigments as well. It is much better to test an idea on a test sheet than on your actual project.

## How to Use Section 3 of Your Test Sheet

The template dedicates an entire sheet for your Section 3 test. That provides plenty of room to try many different things. It is good to practice doing a specific task several times. That will allow you the chance to try different things, side-by-side, until you feel more comfortable about tackling it on the project itself. You can create several test sheets of Section 3 for a project, just as you did for Sections 1 and 2. In addition, some of your ideas and results can inspire other project approaches, especially if you take good notes and keep the test sheets for future reference.

Pull out your line pattern (deer portrait or Koi fish). Look at your reference materials.   Familiarize yourself with the pattern and look closely at how the pattern relates to the reference materials. Look for portions of the image, textures, and items on which to practice.

Choose an aspect to try and go for it! Give yourself permission to experiment and try. You may have never created a deer or fish before; here is your chance to practice. Do the best you can. Repeat with the same item until you feel comfortable with it. Try using different approaches to see what you like.

Let's look at some ideas.

### Section 3 - Deer Portrait Examples

With the Deer Portrait design pattern, practice creating an eye or ear or the nose. Try your hand at creating the textures of the fur, blending colors of lighter and darker shades. Play with ideas for coloring your background.

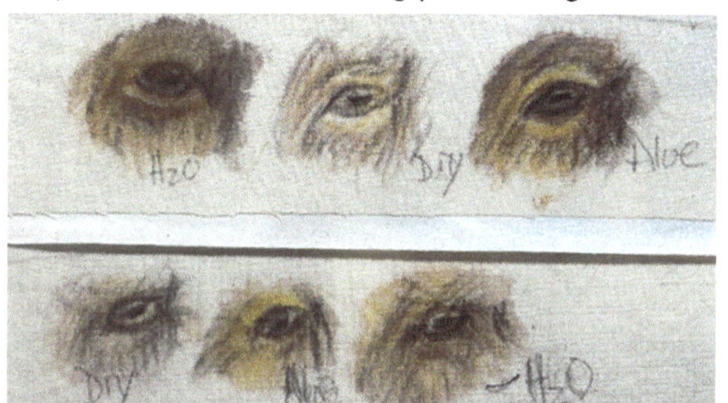

The preceding picture shows some examples of eyes that were created. Notice the short notes on the test sheet, documenting what experimenting had been done with different mediums.

## Section 3 - Koi Fish Examples

If your design choice is the Koi fish, practice drawing and coloring the scales of the fish. Try creating the face of the fish, with the eye(s), the mouth, and the gills. Or try the fins. Start practicing how you want to create the swirls and bubbles in the water.

In the process of using Section 3, you will not only gain experience with what the pigments can do but can begin to think of how to create elements in your design. The scale of your drawing is usually not important; the blending of colors is. Just remember that the size can make a difference in terms of the level of detail that you can achieve. Try all your ideas. You may discover something you really like and want to use on your project. Along with the ideas, you are continuing to gain confidence.

## Create Several Iterations

As you did in Sections 1 and 2, try creating the same item multiple times, using several different methods. You could use dry pigments; and then again wet with water; and then wet with aloe to see which you feel more comfortable with. You may find you like how different techniques look. You can use multiple techniques together when you create your project.

## Observe and Take Notes

Take your time. Explore. Take pictures to capture your progress on a specific aspect. Combine different techniques. Keep good notes, just in case you discover a method that produced results you really liked. That way your chances of recreating it are better. If you really like how something comes together, highlight it and document "why." Outline the steps you took. If something doesn't work out, the same concepts apply. Document the steps that you think worked and the things that did not work as expected. Everything is valuable information to capture. This may help you avoid getting the same negative result another time.

Don't give up if you create something you don't like or you don't feel was successful. Do it again. Each time you do that, you are learning. Give yourself permission to play and learn and try things.

Remember that there is no such thing as a mistake. It is an outcome not expected. You may not like it, but you can learn from it.

Section 3 gives you the opportunity to test how your chosen colors will blend in the design. The results may not be as you expected. You can then try other colors and combinations. You are not limited to using four (4) colors in your project; you can add colors, including black and white, to add details and highlights.

## Your Turn - Section 3

Experiment on your own with your test fabric for Section 3. Review the instructions, if necessary. Look at your pattern and reference materials for ideas. Look at other colors to try. Review your test sheets for Sections 1 and 2 for ideas of approaches to practice. Don't forget to make notes and take pictures!

When you are done coloring your own Section 3, read on for a discussion of this section of the test sheet.

## Observations and Results - Test Sheet - Section 3

What you just did with Section 3 is a very powerful path for learning. Starting out with small elements of your design allows you to develop more confidence in your own abilities. Even if you have never drawn an animal or fish, you can draw portions of one. Then, you simply combine the smaller pieces into a larger composition. What may have felt daunting at first has now been broken down into doable pieces.

The opportunity to try different approaches based on your experience with the test sheets is also powerful. You might never have thought to use aloe had you not experienced working with it first. Blending colors using the mediums can result in wonderful effects as well. The more you are willing to try, the more confident you will be. Section 3 is your practice sheet. Use it.

### *Reflections on Your Testing*

If you completed the testing as outlined, I am confident that you now feel more comfortable and are ready to move forward to your

project itself. These test sheets can be used to experiment using any type of pigment. You are testing pigments before you try to use them on a project. The element of surprise (good or bad) is lessened that way.

If you are considering using several different fabrics in your project, you should do some level of testing with them as well. The advantage to doing this is to become aware of what will happen before you have your heart set on using a specific fabric. It may or may not be appropriate for what you intended. Testing is one way to find out, before you have done a lot of work.

If one type of fabric does not work as expected, but you still want to use something similar to it, see if there are other slightly different variations to the fabric that may work (different thread counts or content). You may also want to try other pigments on that fabric that may work better.

Keep your testing sheets for future reference. There may be a different project in the future for which something you discovered while testing could be a perfect candidate technique for a design.

## Can I Control Wicking?

Some mediums are better at controlling wicking than others. You should have seen the differences between the water and the aloe because of your test sheets. There are other mediums that might help this as well.

Wicking will continue until the fabric dries, so the movement of pigments can go on for a while. If you have added too much moisture, you can try to blot the extra away using paper towels or a blow-dryer. However, you may cause the wicking to progress even further by doing that. The best solution is to control the amount of water/aloe you use from the beginning, so the wicking is minimized.

Is there anything else we can do to better control wicking? Experimenting helps to understand how quickly pigment will wick on a particular type of fabric using a particular medium. Knowing that, you can adjust the amount of moisture (water or other medium) you have on your brush.

Another proactive approach is to apply a wet pigment away from the edge line of the subject you are coloring. The wicking that happens may not spread over your outline. You can use your brush with careful strokes to push the pigment wicking further to move in the direction you want. This will take practice to master, but it will increase your coloring confidence.

### Should I Always Test Before Starting a Project?

Once you have used a specific pigment a lot, you may not need to do as much testing and experimenting because of your comfort level with its use. Keep in mind that every project will be different because of the subject matter, the pigments, and the fabrics used to create it. Testing will always be important to do, perhaps not at the same level as you have done here.

Each section in the test sheet has been designed to serve a specific purpose, and each section provides insight. As you gain experience, the testing may not need to be as formal. You can decide what you need to test. Create your own test sheets based on the project at hand. You may not need Sections 1 and 2 so much.

However, Section 3, or at least the concepts contained in it, is something that will be valuable to do with every project. It will help to define your approach before you commit to the project. It will also allow you to test on a specific fabric, since that can really change the results.

### Other Ways of Testing When Coloring on Fabric

In addition to "formal" test-sheet processes, there are other ways to test your pigments. Plan to include extra "real estate" of the various fabrics on the outside edge of your project. This is beneficial in many ways:

- You can use the extra fabric to test the pigments

- You have the flexibility with the final size of your design, including any shrinkage from heavy quilting

- You won't have to start and stop so much as the extra fabric will give you room to "travel" while machine quilting

Always test your pigments before using them on a project. That minimizes any surprises (such as massive wicking from a tip, dirty tips, surprises in the actual color of the pigment, etc.). There will be many times when you will be very grateful for that! Whatever way you choose, either a formal process or on-the-fly, you now understand the benefits of doing experimenting and testing. The choices are yours to make.

# Part 4: Techniques & Tools: Let's Start Your Project

## Reflections

Let's look back on what you have accomplished so far in your Pigment Patchwork adventure.

- You created test sheets and experimented with various pigments focusing on the project you are planning to start

- You've learned various techniques that you can use on the project and know better how you want to proceed

- You have a better understanding of the key factors that influence how pigments take to fabric and the importance of testing

- You have already grown tremendously in terms of self-confidence in using pigments on fabric

Be kind to yourself. Take a look back at where you were at the beginning of this adventure and give yourself a pat on the back. Look how far you have come. You may still feel a bit unsure with using pigments to color on fabric. That is only human nature. Once you start working on your project itself, your confidence will grow even more.

## Before You Start Your Project – More Decisions

I know you want to get started with your project, but there's more to think about before you begin. Let's do a little more analysis so your confidence level remains high, and you have a game plan to proceed.

## Decision Time!

These decisions are important whether you are using the book's Learning Activities or starting your own project.

### Analyze Results of Testing and Make Design Decisions

Testing and experimenting can be fun as well as educational. You can create multiple test sheets and try different approaches, different

techniques, and get practice working with the pigments. On the other hand, be careful not to get stuck in a rut with testing and not move forward. I call that Analysis Paralysis.

Remember your goal is to prepare yourself to color on the project itself. What kinds of analysis and what decisions will be important to moving forward and not getting stuck?

Here is a checklist of steps to use. Let's look at each step in more detail. The first item in the checklist, what pigments will you use, should have already been addressed with your testing.

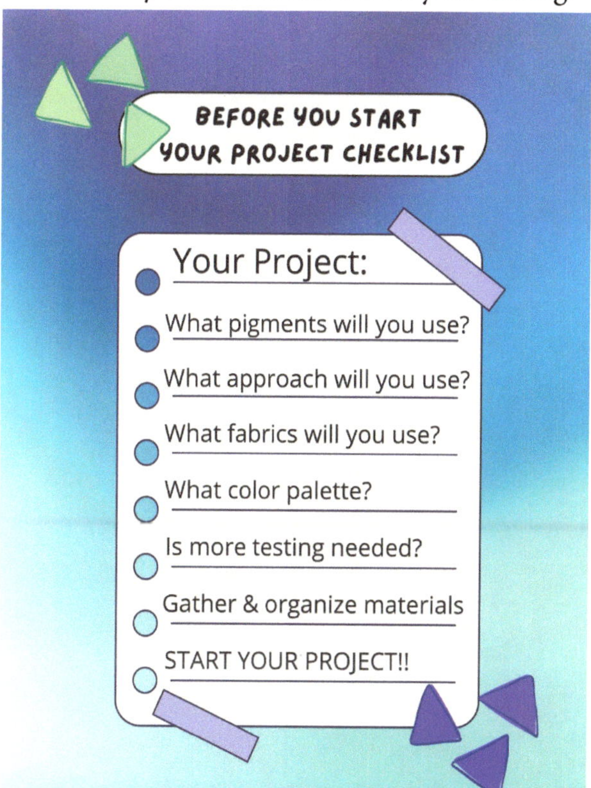


## What Approach?

Based on your testing, you now have a much better understanding of some approaches you take with your chosen pigments. Think specifically about the project at hand (either the Deer Portrait or the Koi Fish from the book Learning Activity, or a project you are planning to make).

Decide how you want to color your project based on what you learned during your testing. Whatever you decide, previous testing is recommended so you feel comfortable with the decision. To help you see some possibilities, the following pictures are samples done using different approaches. This illustrates how different the project can look.

### Sample Approaches - Deer Portrait

Here are examples of the Deer Portrait project.

The three images on the far left used the dry

Inktense pigment. The middle two images were made using the dry Inktense pigment and aloe vera gel. The two images on the right used dry Inktense pigment and water.

### Sample Approaches - Koi Fish

Following are examples of the Koi Fish project.

The three images on the far left used the dry

Inktense pigment. The middle two images were made using the dry Inktense pigment and aloe vera gel. The two images on the right used dry Inktense pigment and water.

After seeing these, you may have a better idea of whether or not you should do more testing before proceeding with your project.

### What Fabrics?

Your final fabric choice may be modified based on your testing results. For the Learning Activity project, you only need one piece of fabric. For other projects, you will decide what fabrics to use, based on your testing. By testing several fabric options, you have the flexibility to change fabrics, knowing which ones will work for the pigments you plan to use.

Here is an example. My project, *Bulldog - The Eyes Have It* (30" x 40"), used a combination of natural silk noil fabric and colored fabrics. I only had a certain amount of brown fabric in the appropriate colors in my fabric stash and,

based on my testing, I knew I could use all of them together to make the dog. I was able to create the design without having to shop for additional brown fabric.

### What Color Palette?

Choose a color palette. Are you considering changing your original color palette decision? You started by testing with the recommended colors listed in the Learning Activity instructions. You had the option to test other colors as well. Before you make a final decision about the color palette you will use for your first project, here are examples of two different color palette options you might consider.

### *Sample Color Palettes - Deer Portrait*

The example of the deer on the left is monochromatic or black-and-white. The example on the right is a more colorful palette. Both were created using a mix of approaches.

### *Sample Different Color Palettes - Koi Fish*

These two examples of the Koi fish were also created using a combination of approaches. The monochromatic one on the left and the colorful palette on the right.

You are welcome to change your color palette decision for your first project. If you decide to change your colors, and your testing did not include them, you should take the time to test the new colors before using them on your project. You will be better prepared to start.

How does this relate to future projects? You may want to plan to experiment with pigments for color palettes during your testing phase unless you know what approach you want to use. You can always do another project of the same pattern using an alternative palette.

## More Testing Needed?

If you decide to consider other color palettes for your project, or want to try out other fabrics, it would be best to do more testing and experimenting before you begin. Your confidence will be much higher when you start and there should be fewer surprises.

## Gather and Organize

With your color-palette and fabric decisions finalized, it is time to gather all your materials. Start out with a clean workspace. Not only does it help you begin with a clear frame of mind, but it also makes practical sense. A clean workspace will minimize any vagrant pigments that could color your fabrics.

Pull out your line pattern and reference materials so they are handy. Gather the base fabric for your project, along with the freezer paper. Get your light box plugged in. Heat up your iron and have parchment paper cut to protect your surfaces. Gather any other materials you think you will need.

## Done with Testing? . . .

If you've decided to change your color palette or think you should do more testing of the colors you plan to use, stop here. Go back, do your testing so you feel confident in your color choices. Then you can move on to the next step. Otherwise, let's move forward.

**Are You Truly Done With Your Testing & Experimenting?**

### *Start Your Design*

Begin by preparing your fabrics and finalizing your design, then transfer your pattern to your fabric in preparation for coloring on your project. Here is a checklist to use for the task of Start Your Design.

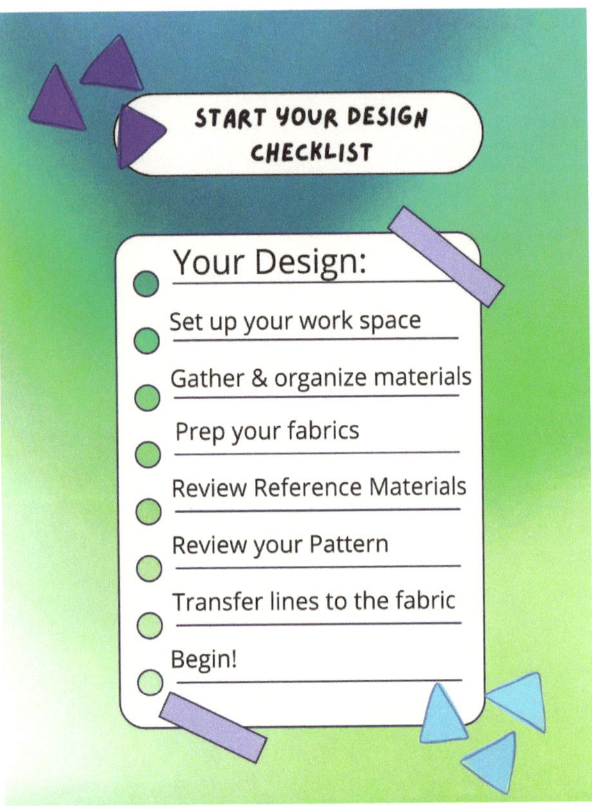


You have already set up your workspace and gathered and organized your materials. Let's talk about the next steps.

### Prepping Your Fabrics for the Project

For the Learning Activity project, cut your washed fabric and freezer paper to a size the same as or larger than your pattern, stabilizing the fabric with the freezer paper.

For other projects, you may want to wait to prep your fabric until you are ready to use it. In the meantime, organize the fabrics you have gathered for this project so you can find what you need for each aspect of your design. Start with your background or base fabric, cut the fabric large enough to fit your pattern, allowing extra space around the edges. Cut the freezer paper (or whatever else you might be using as your fabric stabilizer) approximately the same size or a little smaller. The extra fabric around the perimeter will provide fabric on which to test your pigments before coloring, and a place to clean the pigment tip surface (to remove extra pigments). This area can also be used to remove excess water or other mediums from your brush.

What if the size of your project is very large? If your freezer paper will not cover the entire piece of fabric, iron another piece right beside it. This same approach works for most stabilization methods.

### The Importance of Reference Materials

Next, review the project Reference Materials. Study the reference photos and/or patterns to become familiar with the details. Identify highlights and dark, shadow areas. Look closely at the textures. You did this to some degree earlier, deciding on details to practice for Section 3 of the test sheets. This is similar, but with a different emphasis. Now you are looking at the reference photographs to become familiar with your subject matter.

### Review your Pattern

Your line pattern is a guide for coloring on fabric. It is also a great tool to assist you in putting your design pieces together, especially if you are using an appliqué approach. Look at the pattern lines closely. Compare the line pattern with the reference materials, if you have any. Identify what the lines mean. Where are the major outlines of features of the design? Those are important. The other lines probably represent details, smaller features, textures, etc. In fact, there may be lines you want to add to

the line pattern based on your review of the reference materials or your project objectives.

Most ready-made patterns are made for appliqué sewing projects. They may not have the level of detail needed to assist you with coloring on fabric. You will want to add extra lines to them, either on the pattern itself or on the fabric when you transfer the lines to it. When you make your own line pattern, you can decide what lines to include in the pattern so the details will be there for you.

You decide what lines to transfer from the line pattern to the fabric. The goal is to recreate the shape of the pattern on your fabric, to give you enough of a guide to feel comfortable that you can color. Perhaps you don't need every line. While you are looking at the pattern, determine if there are lines that are not necessary. If there are, don't transfer them. It is that simple. Later, if you determine that you need those lines after all, you can always reposition the line pattern and add them to the fabric. Or, because of your familiarity with the subject matter, you can draw the lines on the fabric yourself.

### The Deer Portrait Pattern

The deer-portrait pattern was created using the included reference photographs of the doe. Familiarize yourself with the pattern lines so you can determine for yourself what lines to transfer to your fabric. Add more detail lines to the pattern if you wish, using the reference photo.

### The Koi Fish Pattern

The Koi fish design is a line drawing for which there was no reference photograph. It was inspired by another design that I liked. I abstracted aspects of the fish and water, making it my own design, so this pattern is more stylized. You can find pictures of Koi fish to get a better understanding of the structure of the fish. Or, you can just have fun creating your own fish.

### Transferring Pattern Lines to the Fabric

### What Lines to Transfer

When you created your pattern for the Butterflies, the process was straight-forward. The pattern was a simple outline. Even with that simple pattern, you had to decide which lines to transfer to your fabric. This same concept applies to any pattern.

How do you decide which lines are important? Your decisions will be influenced by:

- Your study and understanding of the subject matter itself

- Your understanding of what the lines on the pattern represent (by comparing them with the reference materials)

- Your decisions about the project you want to create

- Your confidence level

*Rhonda's Guidelines for Transferring Pattern Lines to your Fabric*

What lines should you transfer?

- In general, start with key lines - the outline of objects. For example, the overall shape of the deer or the Koi fish

- Then consult your pattern and move on to other key shapes inside the overall shape: the eyes, nose (for the deer), the gills (for the Koi fish), details of the mouth, etc.

- Wait to transfer any detail lines until last. It may sound tedious to do it this way, but this allows you to get in tune with your subject matter while you are in the process of creating your pattern on the fabric.

- In fact, when you are working on a project, you will become very familiar with your subject matter because you will recreate the lines numerous times, especially if you have created the pattern yourself.

- The more familiar you are with the subject matter, the more you can bring out its character with your creative voice. Your decisions will be affected by the amount of experimentation or testing you have done.

- Section 3 of your test sheet is specifically designed to help you with that and, as a result, increase your confidence. If you are more confident, you may not need to transfer all the detail lines. Only you can decide. Of course, this depends on the subject matter of the design and your experience.

## Pattern Line Transfer to Fabric - Colors for the Lines?

In most cases, the lines you transfer to the fabric should eventually disappear into the coloring of the subject matter, unless you want the lines to be seen. So how should I make my lines? Thick or thin? What color? What pigments? The following is my advice.

### *Guidelines - What Colors to use for Pattern Lines*

Tips for pattern lines on your fabric:

- Draw the line(s) in a color that is either neutral (gray or light tan) or that matches the line's subject matter (e.g., deer portrait, light-brown; Koi fish, light orange; background lines Koi fish, light blue)

- Note: Using a light color such as yellow or off-white is NOT recommended - unless it is on a dark fabric; those colors are very hard to see and you may regret that choice

- Draw your lines using very light pressure; you want lines that you can see, but that can be easily concealed or covered

- Thin lines are better than thick lines, for the same reason

- Do <u>NOT</u> use a water-soluble pigment to draw your pattern lines; if you use a wet medium, it will react with the lines

## Pattern Considerations for Different Project Approaches

There are at least two different ways to look at how you use patterns, whether it is a pattern you have purchased ready-made, or one you have created yourself. This advice also depends on the approach you are taking with your project, whole cloth vs. appliqué.

## Considerations for Whole-Cloth Project Patterns

For a whole-cloth project, the pattern plays a leading role in your project. It provides you with guidelines for coloring on the fabric. In essence, you need only one pattern for your project. You will transfer the pattern lines to your background fabric and go from there.

***Example 1 of a Whole-cloth Pattern on Fabric - Zebra TEHI***

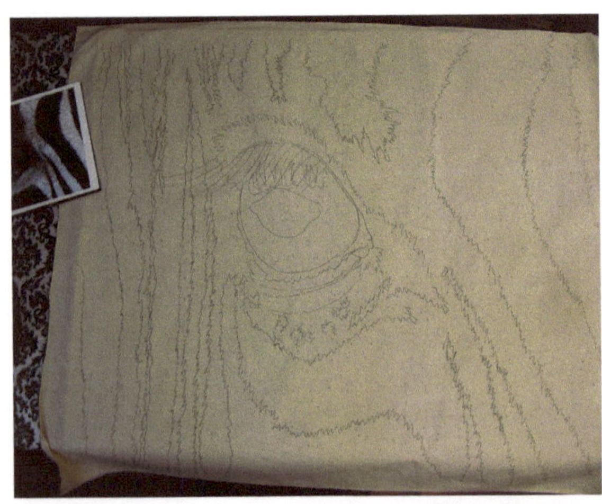

This is the whole-cloth pattern transferred to fabric from my project *Zebra: The Eyes Have It*. The base is a large piece of silk noil fabric (approximately 46" x 36") that was ironed onto multiple freezer paper pieces aligned side-by-side to form a stabilized coloring surface. A light box was used to trace the pattern lines onto the fabric with a mechanical pencil. You can see the lines are light, just dark enough to see them. The reference photo is set next to the fabric as a guide for applying pigment.

***Example 2 of a Whole-cloth Pattern on Fabric - Hans My Hedgehog***

This is a whole-cloth pattern on fabric for *Hans My Hedgehog*, partially colored in this picture. Because of the black fabric, the challenge was to figure out how to see the line pattern well enough to transfer the lines. A light box was not bright enough to see the lines well enough, but a large window on a bright day worked--a bit of a challenge, but it worked out well. It also helped that it was an original design and the wished-for result was known.

A white colored pencil was used to draw the lines. If you look closely at the colored areas, you can see that the white lines blended well into the coloring on the fabric.

**Pattern Considerations for Appliqué**

An appliqué project (either turned-edge or raw-edge) is a little different situation, requiring more than one pattern. One approach is to create an overall Master Detailed Pattern used to create all the pattern segments.

From that master pattern, create an overall "layout" diagram, guiding the placement of the appliqué pieces onto the fabric. For the layout diagram, you only need to transfer an outline of the general

shapes. If you are coloring some of the design directly onto the fabric, you should transfer enough of the detail pattern lines in those areas to use as guidance in your coloring. In that case, your resulting lines on the fabric will be a combination of outline and details, as appropriate.

You will also need detailed patterns for the individual appliqué pieces. The pattern detail lines will be transferred to the fabrics you have chosen to color, colored using pigments, then cut out and appliquéd (either turned-edge or raw-edge) to the background.

***Example of Appliqué Pattern Pieces - Rosemary***

Pictured is the start of an appliqué unit for my project *Rosemary*, created on paper-backed

iron-on fusible and transferred to fabric. After I finished coloring the pattern pieces, they were cut out to be applied to the main project. You can see the reference photos, both small and large, of the girl holding the sheaf of rosemary.

### *Example of Appliqué Master Pattern on Fabric - Rub-a-dub-dub*

*Rub-a-dub-dub* was made using many different fabrics appliquéd onto a base foundation fabric.

This picture shows the layout diagram traced onto the foundation fabric, a piece of muslin.

The lines indicate where the appliqué pieces will be placed in relation to each other. No additional detail is needed on the foundation fabric; that will be on the appliqué pieces themselves. The lines were done in pencil and will ultimately be covered with fabric.

### *Example of Appliqué Pattern Pieces on Fabric - Rub-a-dub-dub*

This next picture shows the tan fabric used for the flesh-tone base. Using the master detailed pattern for the project, the appropriate appliqué pattern sections were traced onto iron-on fusible material, creating smaller

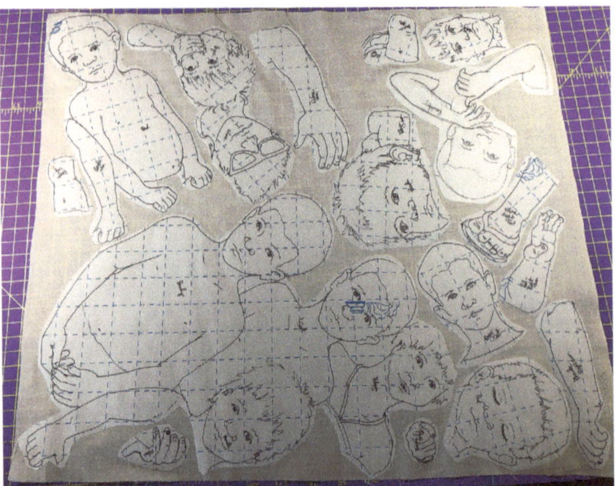

appliqué pieces. The paper-backed fusible material was cut out and ironed onto the wrong side of the tan fabric, leaving room around each piece. This provided spacing to help minimize the impact of potential wicking during the coloring process and room to cut out the pieces. (Note: This explanation is an over-simplification of the process used. It is much more complicated. The concepts are what is important here. This entire process is the subject of more advanced training.)

This is a picture of the front side of the same piece of tan fabric (the ironed-on appliqué pattern pieces on the back). The pattern lines have been transferred to the front of the fabric, using a tan colored pencil, to guide the coloring process.

Leaving the fabric whole gives more stability for coloring than if each piece had been cut out and

colored individually, especially the small ones. It is also easier to see related appliqué pieces that belong together, so flesh-tone colors can be kept consistent. Best of all, there is no worry about losing any small pieces.

***Example of Appliqué Pattern Pieces on Fabric With Some Coloring - Rub-a-dub-dub***

This picture shows the start of adding color to the fabric.

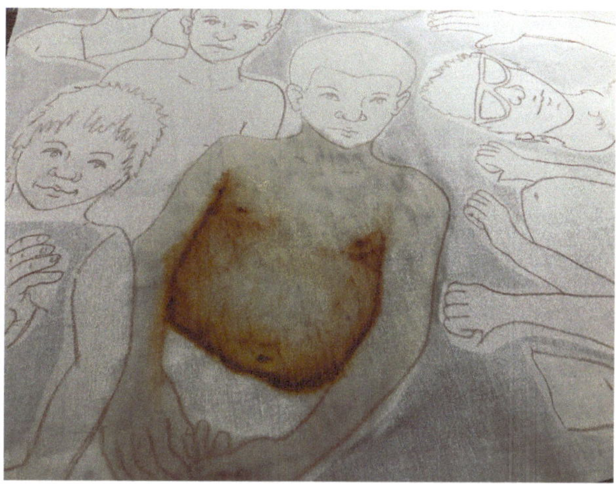

This photo is further along in the coloring process. Some of the groups of pieces have been cut out for easier handling. Notice the fabric

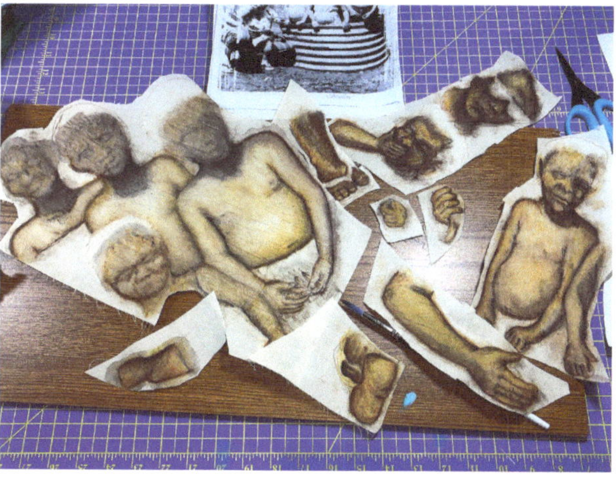

left around the pieces. This will be cut off just before the pieces are added to the design, based on the decision to use either turned-edge or raw-edge appliqué.

Look at these photographs as inspiration. As you continue learning the Pigment Patchwork techniques, these concepts will make more sense to you, if they don't already.

### Your Assignment - Pattern Transfer to Fabric

This is your assignment:

> *Review the pattern and reference materials for the deer portrait or the Koi fish and transfer the pattern lines to create your own pattern on your stabilized fabric/FP unit.*

Once your pattern lines are on your fabric, you are ready to begin your project.

### *Get Ready to Begin*

Everything we have done up to this point is to get you ready for this moment. Give yourself permission to start this step of the process. Let go of any fears or reservations that you may have. You have earned the right to be coloring on this project.

This section will give you some tips and recommendations for proceeding with this adventure step-by-step. Your outline of the pattern is on the fabric. If it is not, stop here and do that. Then you can continue.

### Where to start?

Where to start is a personal decision. You can start with some aspect of the design, say the eyes of the deer or the scales on the Koi fish, and work from there. You can start with a color and go from there.

You can create the main topic of interest first, waiting to do the background after that.

Another option is to start at one corner of the design and move across the fabric. The advantage to this approach is you are not laying your hand in any pigment you may have laid down already. The corner you start on would depend on whether you are right- or left-handed. In any case, you can always lay down a piece of paper or parchment paper to protect your hands from pigment.

There are no hard and fast rules on where to begin. However, you must begin somewhere.

**Tips and Recommendations for Coloring on Fabric**



Let's review some important tips and recommendations for coloring on your project.

1. <u>Take Safeguards Against Pigment Transfer and Smears</u>. From the beginning of your project, keep in mind that the pigment will smear and migrate any chance it gets. So don't let it. Take precautions.

   a. Start with a clean workspace that is protected with plastic.

   b. Start with clean, small containers, clean water, clean brushes.

   c. Keep a moist towel somewhere within reach, but far enough away that it will not get your fabric wet. (Placing the towel on a piece of plastic will keep the moisture under control.)

   d. Keep your paper towels handy.

   e. Wash your hands often.

   f. Heat-set your pigments in your project often (just be aware that it may affect your being able to get the Inktense pencils to "flow" if you do.)

2. <u>Take Your Time</u>. This is not a race. Relax and enjoy the journey. Try to find a rhythm in your work.

3. <u>Don't Push</u>. If you are not feeling good about what you are doing, stop and take a break. Walk away. Take some deep breaths and relax. When you come back, you may find it easier going.

4. <u>Where to Start</u>? Starting with your light colors will usually give you a better feel for what you want to do. Then, take a break, come back, and add some more

pigment, building up your layers of color. This approach gives you the best results and allows the piece to develop. It is always easier to add pigment than take it away. Add shadows and dimension over time with multiple layers.

5. <u>Be Patient</u>. If you are using wet mediums, give the fabric time to dry in between sections, unless it is critical that the entire area looks the same. In that case, you should do a section before stopping. Once the pigment dries, you can always add more pigment.

6. <u>Document As You Go</u>. Use your mobile phone or digital camera to take pictures throughout your project - a step-by-step documentation of your progress. If you do not, you'll wish you had. Be proactive with your photographs; you can always delete some, but you can never capture a moment that is gone. Take notes as you go.

7. <u>Be Aware</u>. There is nothing wrong with continuing to experiment as you do your project. However, if it is something you have not practiced on your test sheet, create a  test sheet and practice what you are attempting before you commit to using it on your project fabric. You won't regret this.

8. <u>Take Breaks</u>. Look at your project from different perspectives. Every now and then, stop, walk around your workspace, and take a little break from coloring. Come back and look at your design from a different perspective,

upside down, sideways, from a distance, etc. Take a picture, use your filter to make it black-and-white and look at it. You may notice things you didn't see before.

9. <u>Dance with the pigment!</u>
   While you are using the pigments, get in tune with the process and what is happening on your fabric. Work with the pigments and the fabric. Enjoy.

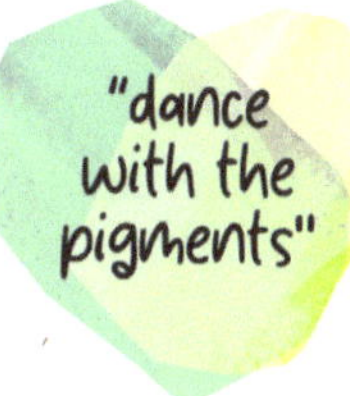


10. <u>Review Progress.</u>
    As you continue working on your project, occasionally stop, review your reference materials and your project. How are you progressing? How are the colors coming together? What was your goal for this project at the beginning? Has it changed? Enjoy the ride.

11. <u>Be Flexible</u>. If your goals or the piece itself have changed into something different, that is perfectly fine. Remember, you need to remain flexible and work with the pigments as you color. Your result may be very different from what you initially expected. And that is okay.

### *Are We There Yet? Am I Done?*

How do you know when you are done coloring on a design? Sometimes that is a very hard question to answer. Remember that the pigments are a part of your design. You do not have to do everything with the pigments unless that is your goal. You have other ways to add to your design, such as:

- Stitching to bring out highlights, dimensions, and details

- Adding more pigments later in the process

- Adding details with embellishments other than pigments

Sometimes you will know when you are done with a phase of coloring and are ready to move forward. Other times, you may want to keep working at something you feel is not quite right. Should you keep going in that case? Only you can answer that.

The next step is reviewing your work. That is in the next section, including suggestions on making possible changes. Do the best you can now. Then you can review the work and make some decisions.

### *Your Assignment - Start Coloring on Your First Project*

It is your turn now. Create your first project. Review this section as needed, then begin. When you feel that your design is ready to review, move on to the next section.

# Part 4: Techniques & Tools: Look What I Created!

### *A Project Ready to Review*

You did it. Your first project has been colored using Pigment Patchwork techniques. You should feel good. This is your first giant step. Regardless of how you feel about the results, you have made great strides.

## *Congratulations!*

### *Looking Back - Successes and Challenges*

Before you go much further, this is the time to reflect on how things worked out on your project. Write some notes while everything is still fresh in your mind. It will help you to remember key lessons and ideas for later projects. It will also help you with this section of the book.

You may feel very excited with everything that happened as you created your first project. There may have been things that were not expected. Perhaps you did not like how some aspects of your project turned out. Don't lose heart. There may be ways to address that. Or you might decide that you like the design after all. We will examine all of that in this section. Everything you experienced is valuable.

Practice makes Progress!

Every art quilting/mixed media project that you do will carry an element of surprise. The more you explore what happened, the more you will be able to predict or anticipate what will happen in your next project. That is where the adventure continues. The biggest challenge with using pigments on fabric is the spontaneity of the result because there are so many factors that can influence it.

Don't forget. You will be finishing this project, so you will add stitching, and that gives you lots of possibilities. You can also add pigments to your work even after you add stitching.

As this Chinese proverb says: What I hear, I forget. What I see, I remember. What I do, I understand.

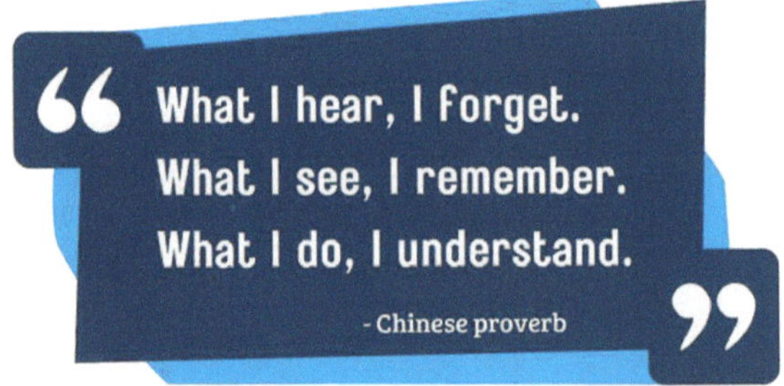


In this section, we will analyze your results so you can learn even more. This is the review process that is used in Pigment Patchwork, an analysis consisting of four questions:

1. What did I like?
2. What worked well?
3. What surprised me?
4. What the heck happened?

### Review Step 1 - What Did I Like?

Start with the question "What did I like?" There are always positive aspects about a project that will be self-encouraging. Positive reinforcement will go a long way, especially when you are learning a new skill. As temperamental as coloring on fabric can be, there is always

something good that happens, even if it is a lesson learned.

Analyze your emotions as well as what happened with the technical aspects. How did you feel? Was it thrilling? Exciting? Scary, but in a good way? Were you proud of what you accomplished? Focus here on the positive aspects first. We will get to the other emotions and aspects in a later step.

What did you like about the actual experience of creating the project? What happened that you liked? What went well? Try to think about the details, it may help with your analysis. Can you determine why something made you feel good? Take notes.

My project, *Lunchtime Secrets*, will be used to illustrate this review process. To keep it simple and focused, details of the project will be kept at a minimum except to illustrate the process and how it was used.

### *Lunchtime Secrets* - **What Did I Like?**

A new pigment and process were used to create the whole-cloth base for *Lunchtime Secrets*. Unfortunately, the initial results were far from satisfactory. However, by asking this question, I was able to refocus on the positive. I acknowledged my disappointment and frustration and then let it go to look at what I liked about the experience. It was exciting to try something new with this project, a new pigment, and a new application process. I found I really enjoyed the learning process and recognized all that I learned.

Note: Initially, you may find it hard to stay positive in this first review step. Remind yourself that you will get to cover the things that didn't go well later. You want to start out on the positive side of things. It will get easier the more you use this analytical approach.

### Review Step 2 - What Worked Well?

Once you recognize the emotions, you can then remove yourself from them to look at what

happened in the project. The next question during this analysis is "What worked well?" Notice the different emphasis?

Did the earlier testing and experimentation you did help you? Did you transfer all the pattern lines that you needed to be successful? Did the results of the colors you selected come out the way you expected, especially when you started blending colors together?

### *Lunchtime Secrets* - **What Worked Well?**

The new dye pigment that was used in this project had some interesting effects on the fabric and, with more experimentation and testing, it could be a coloring approach I would try again. The dye pigment colored the fabric, just not as well as had been anticipated. This added a new pigment application to my toolbox of techniques. I loved how I was able to create the background chalkboard writing and some of the details on the lunch tin and books. There were other positive aspects of this approach, giving me more ideas for other projects to try it with.

### Review Step 3 - What Surprised Me?

The next question is "What surprised me?" Even here, you want to include the emotion aspect, since that is usually a clue to some success or challenge. Was there some aspect of your approach that was surprising to you? Was it something you hadn't expected? Did the pigment behave in an unexpected way? Perhaps it was something that didn't come up during your experimenting and testing phase. It could have been something that was different from what you had already experienced. If this is the case, try to determine what may have caused it.

Many times, this step gives great insight into what happened. In addition to amazement and wonder (a more positive result), it can also include disbelief and shock if it was more negative. These kinds of surprises are a reminder that "things happen" regardless of your preparation and you need to remain flexible. Acknowledge the emotion, then separate yourself from it. Analyze what happened. Try to evaluate what steps you were doing and try to recreate the sequence of events. This can be good or not so good. In either case, you can learn from it.

If you cannot determine what happened, at least try to identify any factors that you recognize and document them. Hopefully, this analysis can help you recreate the effect or avoid it. You might also come up with some ideas about where you could apply it, or even tweak it, to get something different. Sounds like the subject for some additional experimenting and testing.

### *Lunchtime Secrets* - What Was I Surprised By?

The resulting colors on the fabric were a surprise; how different the final colors were from the pigment colors that had been applied! This approach involves a "curing process" and a final rinsing to remove excess pigments. The first time I used dye-painting my colors were very similar.  However, with the sepia colors used in this project, I had to blend colors to produce the tones I needed.

Another surprise was the loss of some of the details once the fabric was rinsed. I did not know much about this new technique, but I thought the dye-paint had dried too fast in some areas even with a covering of plastic. It was difficult to draw any conclusions without more testing. I did realize that the coloring approach is different from what I was used to. I will need to be more flexible and think differently in the future.

Some interesting final effects on the piece were identified. Ultimately, there were good and bad surprises, but nothing discovered would be a deterrent to using this approach for other projects.

### Review Step 4 - What the Heck Happened?

This is the last step in your analysis and where you will address the disappointments that you experienced. This step has been left for last because you need to be supportive of your own skills development. Things that do not go well cannot be ignored, but they can be put in proper perspective. Even when you "hate" what the result was, there is still some good there. All is not lost.

Acknowledge the frustration in what happened, then let it go. Move forward. Separate yourself from the emotion. Analyze what happened, identify the steps and the results if you can. Focus on learning from it. If you were diligent in your note-taking during the process, this will be easier. You may have photographs that show where the problem started. Those pictures can be very helpful.

The goal is to learn from what happened so your chances of repeating it will be fewer. If you don't go through this analysis, you may repeat the same sequence of events that will result in another project that has the same issues.

Most importantly, **<u>Do Not Give Up on the Project Yet</u>**! There may still be a chance to salvage it. I will talk about that in the next section.

### *Lunchtime Secrets* - What the Heck Happened?

Initially, I was very disappointed with the results of the coloring on the fabric. I realized that I did not manage my expectations very well. This was, after all, my first big project with a new process and pigment. After reviewing the results with the group at the retreat, I was advised against using dye-painting to fix the issues for several different reasons. It would be too much of a challenge to even attempt it.

I was told my best option was to use thread painting to fix those areas with which I was not happy. After swallowing my disappointment, I

was able to think more clearly about my options. I realized that my Pigment Patchwork techniques could be used to address the design problems. So, instead of feeling demoralized, I got excited. Without this analysis, I might not have been able to re-evaluate the possibilities and look at the project in a different way. (Later in the book I will explain what I did to fix *Lunchtime Secrets*.)

### Summary – Reviewing your Project Using a 4-step Analysis Process

The key to analyzing the current state of a Pigment Patchwork design project (or, for that matter, any project) is to remove yourself from the emotions. Do not discount the emotions; they can help in your analysis process. Your notes and photographs taken during the creation process are valuable as an aid in determining what happened. And, by adding your notes from this 4-question review process, you will have some awesome resources for future reference.

Unfortunately, you may not always be able to determine what happened, despite the best notes, pictures, and good intentions. That is the upshot. There are so many vagaries and quirks to coloring on fabric. But lessons can still be learned from them. Your basic knowledge of pigments and fabric structure will help you better understand what may have happened.

### Your Assignment - Reflect and Analyze

This is the time to reflect on how things worked with your project. Go through the analysis-process steps. Write your notes while everything is still fresh in your mind. Take pictures of the areas you may be concerned about, showing as much detail as you can. If you make changes to your project, those pictures will allow you to compare the before-and-after results.

After doing this analysis, you may decide that you like your project after all and want to use it without changes. Don't forget - you will be adding thread stitching to your project and that gives you lots of possibilities. You can also add pigments to your work, even after you add stitching.

# Part 4: Techniques & Tools: Can I Fix It?

## *Adjusting Your Piece - Potential Alternatives*

There are ways to restore or correct an aspect of your project that you either don't like or want to improve. Coloring on fabric using pigments can be very versatile. Let's see if there is anything you can do to adjust, improve, or salvage your project.

This is a list of potential alternatives to look at:

- Take a break; take another look
- Embrace the wicking
- Try to adjust the pigment
- Add more pigment, including using different approaches and mediums
- Cut out the project element that is not wanted
- Appliqué over the unwanted project element
- Plan to use stitching to cover and correct the issues
- Treat the project as a study and start over
- Cut up your project and use pieces in future project

More detail on each of these alternatives will be discussed below and illustrated, if appropriate, with one of my own projects.

## Take a Break, Take Another Look

This is the first alternative for adjusting your piece. There may come a point in time when you get so frustrated with your project that you want to throw it into the trash bucket. You are not alone. This can happen to anyone. Sometimes, all it takes is a change of attitude, a break, or a breath of fresh air to help adjust that.

If coloring on fabrics using pigments was so easy, everyone would be doing it. And where is the challenge and fun in that? This "slump" is not something that always happens. If you approached your project using the recommended testing and experimenting guidelines, then you may never feel this way.

If you find yourself at this point, give yourself a break. Walk away and come back to the project after spending time away from it. Do something different for a while, work on other projects. When you come back to the project and take another look at it, you may realize that it is okay after all. Only you can determine how much time away you need. Pieces that are in your work-in-progress pile may fit this situation and may be awaiting your return.

There is still hope if you are not happy with your design. There are other things to try before you give up on your design.

## Embrace the Wicking!

Hopefully, you now understand "wicking" and what it can do to your project. Using the suggestions (outlined earlier in Can I Control Wicking?) may help. Even so, wicking may occur because that is the nature of fabric. When wicking happens, you can either totally embrace it and leave it be, or you can try to adjust or compensate for it. Let's look at embracing it, using one of my projects to illustrate.

## *Wild Rose* - Embrace the Wicking - Leave-It-Be Example

This is a picture of my *Wild Rose* pattern

design. You can clearly see the wicking that took place. I liked the wicking I saw happening when I added the water, but I got carried away with the amount

of water I used. There was nothing I could do to stop it. Still, it had an interesting look and texture.

After the fabric dried, I decided I liked the effect. I added other pigments that were not water soluble to add definition. I did not do anything else with this, but it could be turned into an interesting, finished piece. Instead, I use it in my workshops as an example of embracing the wicking.

## Try to Adjust the Pigment - Potential Alternatives

Another alternative is to adjust the pigment. The possibility of doing this depends on the pigment used, and whether any techniques to "set" the color (ironing or using a medium, etc.) have been used.

Regardless, I recommend you try it. It usually cannot hurt. There are several different ways that pigments can be adjusted on the fabric:

- Dilute
- Blend
- Remove

### Dilute - Adjust the Pigment

Try to dilute the pigment color on the fabric to make it lighter. Both water and aloe have been used to do this, with varying degrees of success. None of the results is optimal, but it may soften the color to some extent. It helps to scrub the area with a stiff brush, cloth, or your clean fingers. You are trying to rehydrate and move the color, soften a hard edge, or remove it as much as you can. You will need to wait until the fabric dries to see just how successful it was.

***Mother Teresa, Let Us Begin - Dilute - Adjust the Pigment - Example***

The following close-up pictures are of my in-progress *Mother Teresa* design. I started coloring the faces but realized I needed to do something with the background. My intent was to create a muted variegated background but I

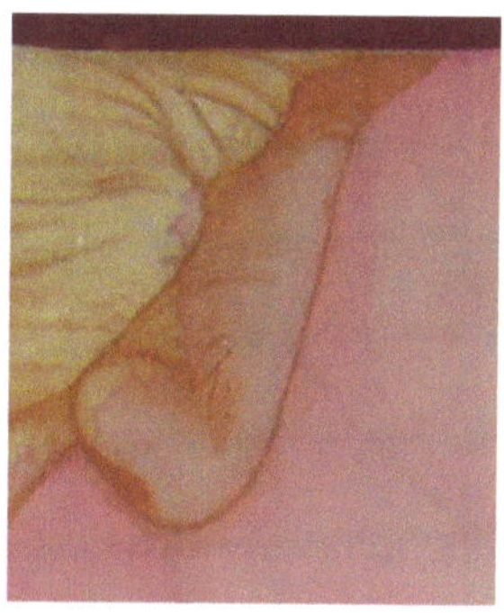

used too much water and the wicking got out of control.

You can see the wicking that carried the pink pigment of the background color into the faces. Luckily, I had only used a light coloring of the background pigments. I used water to try to dilute the wicking end lines (i.e., pigment that is carried by the wet medium and ends up making a line of pigment on the edge of the wicked area). This dilution process was somewhat successful. After the fabric dried, the pink color could still be seen in the faces, but the line of the wicking was somewhat softened. (Note: In my experience, it is very difficult to totally remove the pigment travel line that results from wicking unless you catch this while the fabric is still wet and concentrate on removing the pigment line then. Once the fabric dries, the line stays.) This piece would need additional adjustment.

### Blend - Adjust the Pigment

Blend the pigment on your fabric using either a towel (paper or cloth), a sponge (blending or cosmetic), your clean fingertip, or a special blender stick (called a tortillon or blending stump). Work the pigment into the fabric to blend and soften it. Experiment to see potential results. Blending works very differently on fabric compared to paper because of its composition.

***Deer - Blend the Pigment - Example***

This photograph shows blending and softening of the

pigment in the ear portion of a Deer Portrait sample piece, a dry-pigment project. Realize that the blending tool you use could migrate pigment to other areas of your fabric. Be careful where you place the tool before, during, and after use. The type of pigment you use will also determine how effective this alternative works.

## Remove or Soften – Adjust the Pigment

Try using an eraser (e.g., National – The 500 Eraser) to soften or remove the color. The type of pigment you used will determine how effective this method works. The 500 Eraser can be found in art departments of stores or on-line; other similar eraser brands will work as well. This soft rubber material removes pigment by lifting (removing) it from the fabric.

The removed pigment is either left on the eraser or combined with little rubber shavings. Gently blow or knock the pieces off your fabric, being careful not to color your fabric. Use a damp towel to wipe the eraser clean. You will notice that erasing on fabric is not the same as erasing on paper. In fact, the act of rubbing with the eraser can push the pigment into the weaving structure of the fabric, resulting in bits of color left deep in the fabric structure.

### Deer - Remove or Soften the Pigment - Example

The deer photo below on the left shows an area of the deer cheek (the Before view). The photo on the right shows the effect of having lifted pigment off the fabric using the eraser. Note: the area on the cheek where the pigment was lightened is just to the left of the left-most tip of the eraser.

## Add More Pigment - Potential Alternatives for Adjusting Your Piece

You can also add more pigment to adjust your piece. This is especially effective if you have used a layering approach on your project. There may be times when just the right amount of additional pigment will do the trick to cover up an issue.

### *Mother Teresa* - Add More Pigment - Lighten or Add Highlights

The left photograph is my piece with the wicking showing. The photograph in the middle shows *Mother Teresa's* nose area during the coloring process; the layers of colors are building to cover the wicking. The photograph on the right shows the final piece with the pigments adding lighter tones and highlighting aspects of her face. I was able to cover the wicking so it was acceptable.

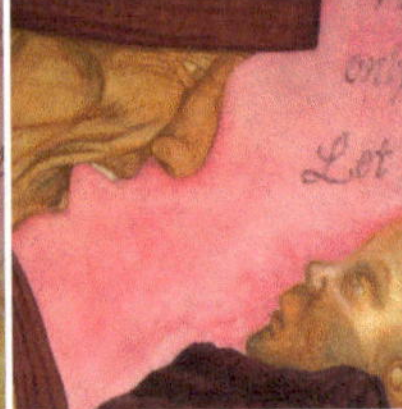

Note: The color differences in these photographs are the result of the lighting used when the photographs were taken.

### Deer Portrait - Add More Pigment - Potential Alternative to Hide Wicking

These pictures show an in-progress Alternate Color Deer Portrait sample piece I was making. On the left, if you look closely, the wicking of the yellow-green color is obvious around the entire deer profile. An aloe medium was used on this piece.

The right photograph shows the use of pigments in the background

and on the deer to cover the wicking. It is not a perfect solution by any means, but this approach can do wonders. Additional layers of pigment could blend it and cover it even more.

### *Rabbit* - Use Different Pigments and Mediums

Depending on the pigments you used in your piece, you may be able to enhance or chance your design by adding different types of pigments or even using different mediums. To illustrate this, here is a picture of a pattern called Rabbit, colored with Inktense dry pigment.

Even though the rabbit could have been left alone, I wanted to see what would happen if I carefully added Aloe to the colored fabric. In this case, I was committed. It might have been better if I tested this option first.

Don't forget, you can use different pigment types and mediums in your design. Just be aware that they may affect each other. Testing beforehand is highly recommended.

### Cut It Out - Potential Alternatives for Adjusting Your Piece

Flexibility is essential when it comes to fiber art. You may start out a project with one approach in mind, say a whole-cloth piece. Later, based on the results of all your efforts, you may decide to change your mind. It is your project. If the situation with your project warrants this approach, please consider it.

Here are some examples to help illustrate this.

### Deer Portrait - Cut It Out - Create an Appliqué - Example

The following are three photographs of different sample deer portraits, each with wicking issues. Water was used on the far left and middle deer portraits, aloe on the right deer portrait.

There are a couple options for taking these designs further and finishing them. To keep the project a whole-cloth, pigments would need to be added to the background to cover or disguise the wicking. Or the deer can be cut out of the fabric, turning it into either a raw-edge or turned-edge appliqué.

Let me show you a real example of one of my projects where I used this approach to fix a major issue.

### Mother Teresa - Cut It Out - Replace a Portion - Example

The picture on the left below is of the piece the first time I finished this project. There was

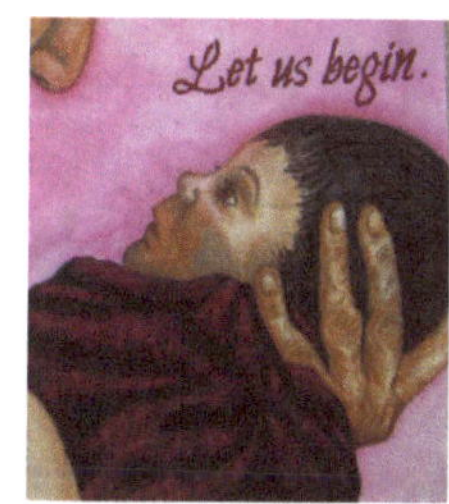


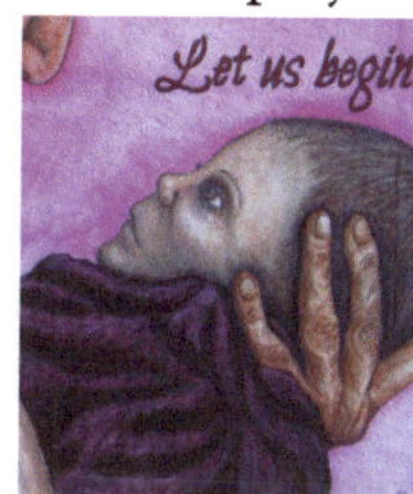


something about it that I did not like, but I had a tight deadline to enter it into a show. I finally realized what was wrong with it when I saw it hanging at the show. The baby's hair was too dark and full; it was not the look I wanted. (I got carried away with the dark pigment for the hair and overdid it.) To stay true to my creative voice, I needed to fix it.

After the show, I removed the stitching on the appliquéd blanket near the baby's face. Then I carefully cut out the fabric of the baby's face and head, keeping the fingers and the background intact. I left a large edge of fabric around the area, allowing me to sew the replacement head back on, covering the area. I created a new head, being careful not to get carried away with the pigments. The new head was slid into place, stitched, and the area re-quilted.

The picture on the right above is the adjusted artwork. If you didn't know what I had done, or hadn't seen the original piece, you might never know. The power of Pigment Patchwork!

## Appliqué Over It - Potential Alternatives for Adjusting Your Piece

By appliquéing something over a section that you don't like, you can hide that area of your project. This is somewhat straightforward, especially if you are a quilter who has done appliqué before. The only thing you need to consider is whether the area you are covering is dark. In that case, you should use some backing material to ensure there is no shadowing.

## Plan to Use Stitching to Cover and Correct - Potential Alternatives for Adjusting Your Piece

You can use thread painting or other embroidery stitching techniques to fix or hide the problems. You will need to finish the top before you do this.

## Treat it as a Study and Start Over - Potential Alternatives for Adjusting Your Piece

In some cases, there is nothing you can do to adequately fix or adjust your piece to your satisfaction. You may have tried some things, and nothing worked successfully.

Treat it as a study - This piece will still be an asset in your project files as a lesson learned. Document your final assessment and keep it with the piece. This is especially powerful if you tried to fix the design and failed. The next time you try this same technique in a project, it may be successful because you benefited from this experience.

Start Over - If you decide to start over and create a new design to replace this one, bravo to you! Before you begin, take a deep breath, and focus on what you are doing. Your previous experience will help you with the next one. We are always learning. Look at this as another adventure. Keep your other design as a study.

## Cut It Up! - Potential Alternatives for Adjusting Your Piece

If you really don't want to save your piece as a study, you could cut it into pieces and reuse it. You could either cut out portions of the piece and reuse them somewhere else. Or you could take the top and cut it into pieces using a rotary cutter or scissors, using a rotary ruler or not. Arrange the pieces any way you want and sew it back together to create something new.

## How I Rescued My *Lunchtime Secrets* Project

This story illustrates how powerful Pigment Patchwork techniques can be. After being

introduced to dye-painting in a short workshop, I attended a multi-day retreat where I focused on learning more of this technique and, in the process, created a design. My goal was to create a whole-cloth piece, approximately 36" x 36", inspired by this old sepia photograph.

There was no dye-powder color that would work right out of the container, so I had to mix my colors, blending various dye powders

together. There was a lot of trial and error, but I managed to create enough for the piece, with very little to spare. Thus, there would be little extra testing.

In the previous photograph you can see my tray with the colors we created, as well as my test sheet in the far-left side of the photo. I used silk noil (raw silk) as my base fabric. I am dye-painting part of the background chalkboard. You can see the plastic covering to retard drying and curing too soon.

This photograph shows my project in-progress. With a limited amount of pigments to use, I started by painting the tin cigar box to get a feel for the process. Then I painted the chalkboard behind the two girls. I worked my way from the top left corner, down and over.

The photograph on the left is my finished dye-painted piece before it was rinsed. Notice the rich pigment colors. I was very excited and couldn't wait to see the results. I had to wait until the piece cured and then I could rinse it to see the final design.

The photo on the right is my project, rinsed out and dry. Quite a difference in color and detail. The group did a show-and-share at the end of the retreat and they tried to help me understand my options at this point.

I know now that this is the nature of dye-painting. There are many unknowns in the process. I was told I had two options at this point:

1.  Attempt to replicate the dye colors and add more dye paint. I was warned the chances were slim to recreate the colors to match, and the colors might not even take to the fiber in the fabric. I was discouraged by the group to even attempt this.

2.  Use thread painting to define the details that washed out or were not added during the dye- painting process.

They did not know about my Pigment Patchwork techniques! Let me show you some examples of how I used my Pigment Patchwork techniques to rescue this piece.

The before picture of the shoes is on the left. On the right is how it was fixed using a combination of pigments. Note: The vertical line in the photographs is a fold line in the fabric and the resulting shadowing.

In this next set of pictures, you can see another issue I addressed using pigments. The first picture is the before picture of an area of my piece that I wanted to work on.

When I examined the dye-painted design carefully to identify what I wanted to fix, I thought I had missed some critical lines in my master pattern; there was no bottom rail to the chalkboard. A closer look at the photograph

showed nothing there; the chalkboard went from floor to ceiling. So, I didn't miss anything, but it didn't look right to me.

There was also a large, ugly dark blob on my fabric, in the corner above the books. (I don't know how that got there!) What could I do to fix it? I decided to add a bottom railing on the blackboard and turn the dark blob into the chalkboard cleaning cloth. Any other dark spots could be scuff marks on the wall.

This photograph shows my-progress in making the fix using pigments to color on the fabric. I am adding color to correct my design. You can see the outline of the bottom rail of the chalkboard, two pieces of chalk, and the rag. It took many layers to accomplish this, but I really liked the results.

This photograph is the results of my coloring on the fabric. Problems fixed.

Here are my before and after photos of the entire design. I was able to fix issues and add more details and definition to the fabric. Because I had my Pigment Patchwork skills in my toolbox, I was able to rescue my project and keep it a whole-cloth piece.

I hope this example provides you with some inspiration. You, too, will be able to do this sort of thing with a little more practice. Your confidence in your own abilities with pigments is growing. Keep up the good work. I hope that you see that the possibilities are endless. You are learning some very powerful techniques to add to your toolbox of art quilting skills. Remember

- Practice Makes Progress! We are always experimenting and learning!

### *Your Assignment (optional) - Adjust things you don't like in your project*

Did you get excited about one or more of the Alternatives to Adjusting your project covered here? If so, this might be a great time to look at your own project(s) and explore making additional adjustments.w

This is totally optional. If you do decide to proceed, remember to take detailed notes, along with before, in-progress, and after photographs so you will have great reference material. You can do it.

We are far from done with your project. You have made great strides in embellishing the fabric using pigments. There are many steps ahead to complete your project. I cover those in the next section.

By the way, these approaches to fixing issues can be used anytime as you develop your design using pigments. You don't have to wait to use them until you are "done" with your design. I waited to suggest this until now, after you created your first design. You now have experience with some of the behaviors of pigments on fabric. You can better understand how the techniques outlined here can be tools to use in your design process from the very beginning, fixing things as they occur.

## Where to From Here

### *Finishing Your Learning Assignment Project*

Now that you've spent time coloring on fabric, it is time to take your project and make it into a finished piece. What can you do with it? Here are some ideas:

- Frame it and hang it on the wall

- Incorporate it into a wall hanging

- Sandwich or layer it, quilt it, put a finishing edge on it, and display it

If you are going to frame your colored fabric piece or incorporate it into a wall hanging, you should iron the fabric one last time to flatten it and set the pigments. If you want to create a finished piece using your colored fabric, there is more work to be done.

There are plenty of resources on the process of making an art quilt, with detailed steps and techniques that you can reference, if needed. From a Pigment Patchwork perspective, however, you have fabric that has been colored using pigments that you want to use to create a finished piece. Will that affect some of the finishing steps you need to perform? This section highlights finishing steps and advice on things to consider when you use Pigment Patchwork techniques. Examples of my own work will help illustrate my points.

### *Tips on Finishing Your Project*

You may already have ideas about what you want to do to finish your project. There are many different options. My suggestions, tips, and recommendations are at a conceptual level, tied to the key steps in creating a finished art quilt.

You will want to finish the piece, so it represents your own creative voice. My goal is to provide thoughts to consider so that your time and effort with the coloring process is enhanced during the finishing process including:

- Assembling, including creating appliqué pieces and units and applying them to the background

- Sandwiching or layering the piece so it is ready to be stitched together

- Enhancing the piece, adding stitching to secure the layers and to add details and definition

- Finishing the piece so it can be displayed

### Assembling the Project

If your project is a whole-cloth design, go directly to the next section. If you are using an appliqué approach, you will have to assemble all the pieces to create the design for your quilt top. I will focus on things to consider when creating your appliqué pieces and adding them to a background. I will also include tips for using pigments to color other areas of your piece, not just the appliqué pieces.

### Appliqué Tips and Recommendations

Three different types of appliqués can be used: Turned-edge, raw-edge, and reverse. My suggestions apply to all of them, used as appropriate.

*Tip 1: Use iron-on fusible instead of freezer paper to stabilize the fabric.*

Paper-backed iron-on fusible usually works well with Pigment Patchwork techniques, even for large appliqués, saving time. There is less handling of the fabric, and it helps minimize fraying.

*Rub-a-dub-dub* - These are pattern pieces for the children, traced onto paper-backed iron-on fusible, ready to be placed on the flesh-tone fabric.

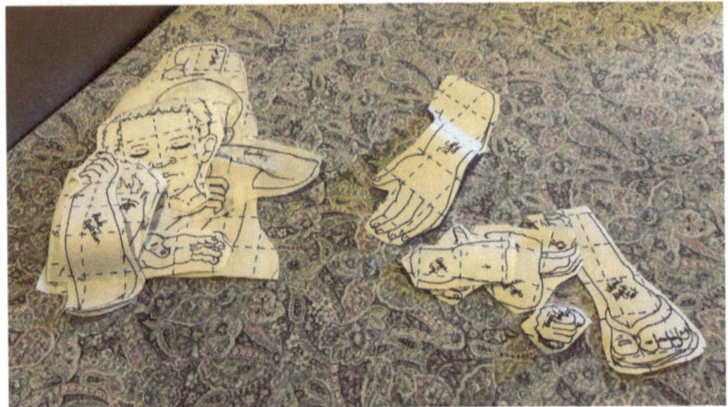

***Tip 2: Plan your layout of appliqué pieces on your base fabric; leave space.***

Leaving extra fabric around your pieces gives you options later in your project. This advice also pertains to how you create your appliqué units, whether they are created together, so they are colored as one; or if you will create each piece separately and put them together later as a unit.

Both situations are illustrated in my *Rub-a-dub-dub* project. Here you see the fusible pieces being laid out on the fabric to be ironed. Not only do the fusible pieces have extra space around the outlines, when the pieces are positioned for ironing, extra space around the pieces is considered as well.

You can also see where a larger piece of fusible was created with four children standing together. This could have been created as four

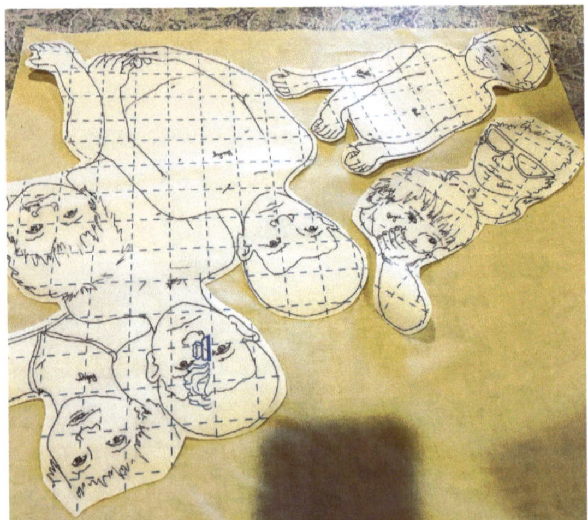

separate pieces (each child) and assembled after coloring. You will need to decide on the approach you will use. If you encounter challenges during the coloring process, you can always change to the other approach.

***Tip 3: Color further outside your pattern lines.***

The goal of this strategy is to give you flexibility for your edges. In this picture, you can see color has been added to the fabric for the body of this boy.

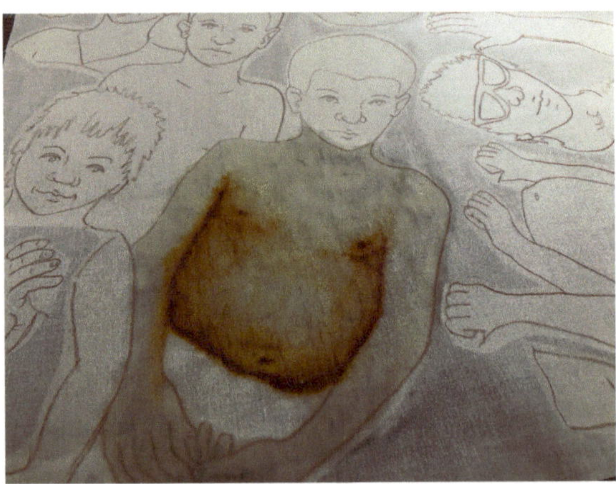

On the right side of the appliqué, where the body outline will be cut out and either used as a turned-edge or raw-edge appliqué, the coloring has been extended to the outline and a little beyond. On the left side, where the subject is one of four children that compose one piece of appliqué, I had to be conscious of those bodies and color appropriately. This tip should be applied judiciously to give you design options later in the process.

Layers of color are used to develop dimension and texture. Be careful using wet mediums for colored edges next to each other (e.g., this same group of children in this picture). Wicking will happen. Experimentation and practice will help develop your skills in managing the wicking as best as possible. Or use the other option of creating each of the children separately and appliquéing them together.

***Tip 4 - Leave extra fabric around edges for turning.***

If you want the crisp look of turned-edge appliqué, you must factor that into your layout. Don't cut yourself short on fabric around your edges.

This picture shows portions of the appliqué pieces of *Rub-a-dub-dub* cut apart from the full fabric piece, with extra fabric around the pieces.

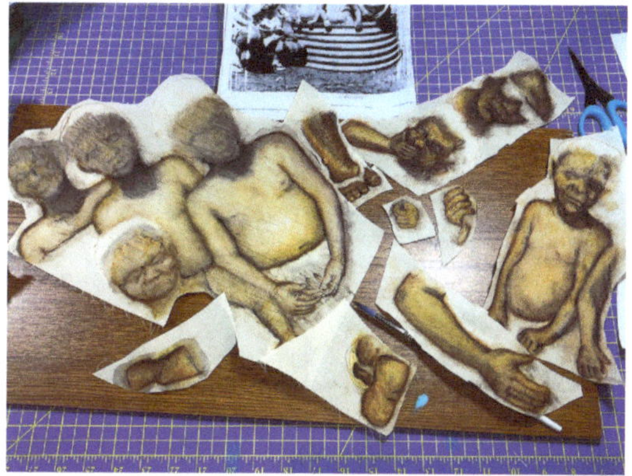

This leaves finishing options open until later (e.g., turned-edge or raw-edge appliqué).

In *Buzzing with Bees*, the girl appliqué piece is laying on top of the quilted top background.

If you look closely at her pink dress, you can see that it is fused to her body with the edges turned under. The white you see around her body is extra fabric left around her arms and shoulders so the two appliqué options will be viable when I get ready to fuse her to the project top.

***Tip 5 - Finish coloring the pieces before you turn the edges.***

Remember that texture of any kind will affect the pigment coloring process. If you turn an edge on a piece, and then add more pigment to color the fabric, there is a good chance you will get a line from the turned edge and the extra layer of fabric underneath. If that happens, it will be a challenge to blend it. It is best to avoid it if you can.

***Tip 6 - Be aware of potential shadowing of fabrics.***

Will you need an extra layer? If you are adding lighter appliqué pieces on top of darker fabrics, this may be an issue.

In *Rabbit - Winter Early Morning Light*, a dark-brown fabric was used to create the rocks underneath the covering of snow. This picture shows the raw-edge reverse appliqué technique

used. I was not concerned about the shadowing you see there. Much of it would be covered by the rabbit appliqué piece.

The remainder of the shadowing would be modified by the pigment coloring used. I was able to blend any shadowing from the darker fabric behind the snow, so it looked natural. What is left looks like a shadow or the rock showing underneath a light coating of snow.

My other option would have been to use another layer of light fabric around the edges. I didn't even consider that here. By the way, that big white spot in the middle is where the rabbit will be placed. You will

see the finished piece later in the book.

## Other Areas to Color? Tips and Recommendations

You are not limited to using pigments to color only the appliqué pieces you attach to your project. There are many options for using pigment to add details, as well as shading to the background and foreground areas of your fabric. The pigments can help define perspective (angles, depth, and distance) through shading. You can augment the pigments with stitching and embellishments as well. I will use pictures from my projects to illustrate my tips for this section.

### Tip 1: Plan.

When you want to use pigments to add shading to background and foreground areas in your pieces, the key is to plan so you are aware of what you want to do.

### Tip 2: Think about timing and layers.

Depending on the details and/or shading or coloring you want to add, the layout of other pieces on the project may be affected. The timing for adding color, in terms of the placement of appliqué units, can be important.

To illustrate this, let's look at my *Rub-a-dub-dub* project in progress. This photo shows the appliqué pieces assembled as a unit and ready to secure to the background fabric.

The fabrics are pinned onto the background fabric so I can finalize where I will place them and mark their location so I can put them back in place later.

This detailed photo is the same project later in the process. The appliqué units are stitched down and secured. The background has been quilted and stitching has been added to the appliqué pieces for dimension.

Notice there are shadows underneath the woman and child, as well as the water trough; dimension added by using pigments. The shading looks as though it is under the appliqué pieces, which it is.

How was this done? I determined where my pieces were going to lay on the background fabric. My master pattern helped there, but more importantly, I used my assembled appliqué units as a final gauge of where I wanted them placed. I marked the location underneath the pieces so the lines would be hidden once the appliqué pieces were put back in place. The appliqué pieces were removed and the fabric colored, so it flowed from under the planned location of the pieces. The appliqué units were placed on top, fused, and stitched to secure them.

### Tip 3: Use pigments to help create perspective.

Coloring with pigments can also help define proportions, angles, depth, and distance through shading. Looking back at the same set of *Rub-a-dub-dub* project pictures, can you see where pigments were added to color the ground, adding dimension and shading? There are detailed bits in the foreground such as rocks and stones and ground contours. It makes the piece that much more interesting and realistic.

***Tip 4: Use pigments to blend and camouflage.***

In *Rub-a-dub-dub*, I had the challenge of having only a limited amount of the foreground fabric I wanted to use. Thinking creatively, I figured out how to use the fabric to cover the area, but  it required using cut pieces together to cover the space. Looking back at the earlier pictures under Tip 2, you can see the layout plan in the first picture. The fabric pieces are pinned (see the yellow tops on the pins) to ensure I was able to cover everything. The resulting patterning from these disparate pieces of fabric really showed up.

I had confidence that I could use my pigments to blend and camouflage the areas when I added my foreground perspective details. In this case, the pigments were used to create dimension, blend, and camouflage the disparate fabric patterns. The second picture shows the results of my coloring.

***Tip 5: Don't forget the other options.***

You can augment the pigments with stitching to help with dimension. Embellishments can work as well. Those will come later in your project. In addition, remember that you can add more pigment at any time during your process.

Let's assume that your top is done, regardless of your approach. Your whole-cloth project is complete and ready. Your appliqué top is complete and ready with the appliqué pieces secured (either by fusing or stitching or both). You want to proceed with the finishing process. What is next?

## Sandwiching / Layering Your Project

Studio Art Quilt Associates (SAQA) defines an art quilt as "a creative visual work that is layered and stitched or that references this form of stitched layered structure." This definition reflects much more flexibility and freedom than most definitions of quilts. The basic concepts of the layers are an important part of either a traditional quilt or art quilt. Sandwiching or layering is the next step in assembling your project. Whatever term you use, there are things to think about.

NOTE:  I do not want to discount any stitching that is done to secure pieces to the top portion of your piece (also referred as the quilt top). That is an important step, but I am not discussing that here.

## Sandwiching / Layering your Project - Things to Consider

***The Innards***

The first thing to consider is the inside material that you are adding to your piece. Batting can be composed of different materials, as well as various thicknesses. Substrates such as felted materials and interfacing materials can be used as inside materials. With SAQA's art quilt definition, anything you do that "references" or gives a "suggestion" of a form of stitched and layered will suffice. So, another layer of fabric could also be considered as valid inside material.

How do you choose what to use? It depends on the look you want to achieve. For the sake of terminology, I will refer to this middle section of your piece as the "innards."

***What Size Ratio to Use?***

What size should your innards and backing be? I am not talking about the finished piece size, although this relates to that as well. I am talking about extra materials around the outside edges of your project. That area supports many aspects of your finishing steps. The big question is, should 

your innards and backing materials be the same size as your top that you created?

For the top layer, it is my best practice to add at least 1 to 2 inches to each side of the project top. That extra fabric "real estate" can be used for many things. If you already have extra fabric incorporated into your top, make the other two layers the same size as the top. If prior planning did not happen, and there is no extra fabric at the edges on the top, make sure the innards and backing are at least 1 to 2 inches larger than the top all around the edges.

Extra fabric can be used as a corridor for traveling with your sewing machine stitching as you move around on the project (more about that in the next section, Enhancing the Layered Structure). It also provides flexibility should you need or want to change the size of a project to compensate for assembly challenges. That will be covered in the next section as well.

### How to Secure the Layers?

You made your composition decisions and your sandwich/layers have been assembled. How should you secure the sandwiched piece, especially if you have used pigments to color the fabric. There are several different ways to accomplish this. Does it make a difference which one you use?

Your choice may be determined by the size of your sewing machine throat space. You should use a method that will survive any required handling of the project while sewing on it, and one that will ensure that pieces do not move position, unless you intentionally move them yourself. It is very frustrating to quilt a piece only to find that units on the top have shifted position without discovery until near the end of quilting. The fix would require removing the stitching, repositioning the pieces, and re-quilting. You want to avoid this, if possible.

When you are using pigment-colored pieces of fabric in your design, the wear from handling and the sewing machine presser-foot movement factors in even more. I tack or sew down any

appliqué pieces to hold them in place, even if I am using a large-throat sewing machine. That lets me concentrate on my quilting instead of worrying about pieces moving.

### Cut to Size Now?

Should I cut my project to size now? Though it may seem like an appropriate time to do that now, especially if you have things sandwiched/layered and secured, that may not be the wisest thing to do.

There are still things you will do in the finishing process that may change the size. My recommendation is to leave it alone for now; do not cut or trim anything yet. If a ragged edge is bothering you, trim it off. Keep the extra materials so you have more options down the road.

## Enhancing the Layered Structure

There are things you can do to enhance the coloring on fabric that you have already done, specifically stitching (quilting). One of my

favorite threads to use for quilting my Pigment Patchwork projects is monofilament threads, either clear or smoke (a gray tint). If you are not familiar with monofilament threads, they most closely resemble the look of fine fishing line and have become easier to work with as the manufacturing technology of these threads has improved tremendously since I first started using them years ago.

Generally, people who have tried using mono-filaments either love them or hate them. A lot depends on whether your sewing machine can use them to sew well; in some cases, it takes some machine setting adjustments. If you've tried using the monofilament threads available more than 10 years ago and didn't like it, you

might want to try using the newer monofil-ament threads available today. You might be pleasantly surprised.

Monofilaments are often a good choice because the thread color does not cover or hide the coloring on the fabric. Your stitching can add definition and dimension. I also like the shine of the threads on the piece.

Other threads can be used as well, the color based on your subject matter: Solid-color threads, as well as variegated threads, are available in several different brands or from different manufacturers. Each one has its use, based on your creative voice. You decide what you want to use. Like the pigments, experimenting and testing will help you determine what threads and how you might use them.

Let's look closer at some stitching options and terminology.

## Stitching Approach Choices

You may have already used stitching (piecing or applique stitching to secure your design elements onto the top layer. Additional stitching is used, not only to hold the layers of your project together, but to add other aspects or elements to your project. You should carefully consider how you want to use your stitching to support your creative voice. This could be to blend the existing stitching work or enhance your design.

How will you stitch on your project? If you are planning on hand-stitching, then your thread choices may be very different than if you are using a machine to do your stitching. I prefer machine quilting, so that is my emphasis in this book. By no means am I discounting hand-stitching; I just don't use it much right now in my own creative journey.

*Stitching Techniques Terminology - My Definitions*

Terminology can be a huge challenge when it comes to stitching techniques. Terms are important to help communicate

ideas, methods, and techniques, but I've found multiple definitions for the same word or phrase. For clarity's sake, I will define and use my own terms for the book. These terms differentiate between the types of stitching techniques used on layered art quilts. The same effects can be created by hand-sewing.

- <u>Quilting</u> - joining layers together by sewing stitches in patterns or lines

- <u>Thread sketching</u> - drawing an outline, shape, design, or picture with stitching, often minimalistic; usually done to secure appliquéd pieces on the piece if not done earlier, or to add to that stitching

- <u>Stitching for dimension</u> - or creating dimension with stitching - my own term to describe my techniques for stitching on art quilts; somewhere between thread sketching and thread painting, but not embroidery.; defined as "adding stitching to help define shapes and dimensions, including dense stitching to 'push' areas of the quilt into the background"

- <u>Thread painting</u> - involves heavy stitching to create designs that look like paintings; often a combination of short and long stitches of hundreds of colors of thread that blend, like painting; the resulting design appears realistic and 3-dimensional

- <u>Embroidery</u> - a combination of thread sketching and thread painting; hand/machine embroidery is more formal; free motion is less formal

Following are some tips and recommendations that are related specifically to your stitching on your project. Whatever technique you plan to use, these tips should apply. If you think about them and plan, you will be better prepared and able to create a wonderful, stitched project.

***Rhonda's Quilting Tips and Recommendations***

My quilting approach is very project specific. I change my approach based on my subject matter, or even how I feel about the project. Sometimes I want to experiment, so I try something different to see what will happen. I always learn something with each project I do.

I have two major methods in my quilting approach, with variations:

- Quilting in stages
  - » Quilt the background, appliqué added afterward
  - » Quilt edges before layering the appliqué
- General quilting

Each method/variation is described along with pictures for illustration.

### Quilt in Stages

Two approaches can be taken to building and quilting in stages:

- Background quilting, appliqué added afterward - Sandwich and quilt the background, then add appliqué pieces and units on top, building the layers of the composition, stitching to secure them
- Quilt edges before layering the appliqué - Quilt around the edges of an appliqué's location, then secure the appliqué; add other areas as needed; when all the pieces are in place, quilt the open sections of the piece.

*Background quilting, appliqué added afterward; Example - Buzzing with Bees*

I decided the composition details for this project were so complex that it would be a real

challenge to quilt after it was assembled. I broke it into stages, building the pieces as I went.

1. Background quilting, appliqué added afterwards - I decided to quilt the background first (making it larger than my anticipated finished size) avoiding areas where large appliqué units would

be placed. This photo shows the background already quilted, with the girl appliqué sitting on top. The dress is sewn onto the body, using turned-edge appliqué.

In this picture, stitching is added to secure portions of the girl appliqué to the background using turned-edge appliqué. No detailed quilting has been added yet.

2. Layering the appliqué - The piece was planned in layers. Where layering was critical, such as the flowers behind her arm and hand, the piece was not stitched down. I stitched pieces wherever possible to ensure they did not come loose during the quilting process. My domestic sewing machine throat space size was small. I really had to manipulate the sandwiched piece to get it under the sewing needle. This build-in-stages technique was very helpful.

Look closely at the flowers and the hand in this picture. You can see where

portions of the girl's hand appliqué were left unsewn. That allowed me to tuck some of the flower appliqué pieces in front of her fingers, and underneath her thumb to provide the proper perspective.

Here, you can see that the hand is stitched down with its turned edges. More flowers were added in layers. The edges were sewn to ensure that nothing moved once I had it in place and fused.

3. <u>Quilt the appliqué and add pigment</u> - Quilting was added to put texture on the flowers and the girl. If you look at her

face, you can see where more pigment was added to enhance the coloring on fabric. I was slowly adding dimension to the piece

with my quilting. I continued, using this approach, to create the quilted top.

The other quilt-in-stages tactic I use is called "Quilt edges before layering the appliqué." Pictures of *Rub-a-dub-dub* are used to illustrate this approach.

<u>*Quilt around edges, then secure appliqué; Example - Rub-a- dub-dub*</u>

The entire background is not quilted ahead of time; instead, the background areas around the planned location of my appliqué are quilted. Then the appliqué units are placed, fused, and stitched to secure them. This helps the quilting stitches look more continuous. I can then quilt the rest of the piece.

The following photo shows the piece being stitched using my sit-down, long-arm sewing machine. The sewing needle head is visible, as well as my quilting hoop

(the black ring), made by Martelli Enterprises. The quilting hoop holds tension and allows me to move the fabric under my sewing machine needle as I quilt. I marked the background so I would know where the appliqué unit(s) will be placed, allowing me to quilt around the area before I secure the pieces to the background. The white on the left is my base fabric.

In this picture, the appliqué units were fused down to hold them in place. Stitching will be added to secure them to the background.

**Rhonda's General Quilting Tips and Recommendations**

My quilting-in-stages is one way to approach quilting a project. Otherwise, I follow more of a general approach. I define three stages, adjusted as needed, depending on the project:

1. <u>First Stage - Secure components</u> - I secure my subject matter components (usually my appliqué pieces and units assembled from appliqué pieces - note that this can be done earlier when the top is being created, during this step, or a combination of the two) to the top. Normally this is done by stitching their edges. If there is a concern that more areas need to be secured, I will do so. I don't want things to move as I stitch.

2. <u>Second Stage - Add quilting to secure components and overall layers grid</u> - I add quilting areas spread out over the surface not covered with stitching. This secures the layers so wrinkles are not introduced during the quilting process and the piece handles quilting shrinkage evenly.

3. <u>Third Stage - Add detail quilting</u> - I come back and start adding detail quilting. Even then, care is taken to keep the level of quilting detail consistent across the piece to minimize potential bunching and distortion. This continues until the stitching is complete.

Some pictures of *Golden Moments* should help illustrate this approach.

This first picture shows coloring on the fabric background by the dog's foot on the right. There is one large appliqué unit: the girl and the dog. When it was ready for stitching, the appliqué unit was secured to the background. My Martelli Bella Sedere sewing machine, with its large throat, was used, so I only needed minimal securing stitches. Then my general quilting approach was used to ensure even stitching across the entire piece.

This second picture shows the finished art quilt. *Golden Moments* was my first art quilt sewn using my sit-down long-arm sewing machine. What a difference the size of the sewing machine throat makes. My Martelli Bella Sedere is my "go-to" sewing machine for larger projects.

**More Quilting Tips and Recommendations**

Here are a few more tips and recommendations:

- <u>You can always add more pigments to your project even after you have quilted it</u>. I added more pigments after quilting in Buzzing with Bees. Normal handling of the piece during quilting or sewing machine presser-foot movement can cause pigment color to slough off the fabric surface. Simply add more pigment.

- <u>You can add more appliqué after quilting</u>. Additional appliqué units can be added to the piece anytime. Stitch them down to secure them. Embellishments

should be added toward the end of the assembly process to ensure they are not compromised. Or switch to hand-sewing.

## Finishing your Project

Your piece is assembled and enhanced with stitching. Now what? Here are some recommendations for sizing your piece, finishing the edges, and adding any finishing touches.

### *Sizing and Trimming Options - Tips*

The following tips are from lessons I've learned related to activities during this step of the finishing process.

### Flatten the Piece

This is also called "blocking." Before you consider doing any trimming, ensure your piece lays flat (unless you don't want the form to be flat). Your goal is to create a flat piece, with no ripples or distortions, for measuring and cutting.

Flatten the piece by ironing or, if the components cannot handle heat or steam, by using a large flat board or surface and weights (heavy items) laid on top. Some quilters recommend wetting the piece, stretching it out evenly using pins to hold the edges, and letting it dry.

Unfortunately, because of the pigments used to color the fabric, this approach may cause problems, so it's not generally recommended. Even the use of steam during this step may cause wicking, so be careful. Heat only may be the best option. As an added benefit, this step reinforces the "fixing" or "setting" of the pigments.

### Sizing Tips - Consider Edge Finishing Options

Think about the edge-finishing options you want to use before you trim the piece. Your

choice may affect the size requirements. More detail is in the Edge Finishing Tips section.

### Trim Using a 2-Step Approach

I recommend you trim your piece using a 2-step approach, unless your finished size does not matter. This method

works regardless of the final shape you want.

First, determine what cut measurement the final project needs to be. Add an extra ¼" to ½" for each side to that measurement and cut the edges to that size. That gets rid of all the extra fabric around the edges and makes the piece easier to handle and to do the final cutting.

After trimming, iron and flatten the piece again, using heat and steam (optional depending on your pigments). Re-measure to the final cut measurement size, carefully marking your lines and trimming off the extra fabric. You are now ready for your edging. This may sound like a lot of extra work, but this 2-step approach catches any issues with sizing your piece. It has saved me numerous times on my projects.

I also use long rulers to measure and mark my fabric before cutting, measuring at least twice before cutting. I use the recommended techniques of measuring to verify that my piece is square if that is my goal. This means that all your corners are cut square at a 90° angle and all edges are cut straight. Your work will look professionally made if you take care to do this.

I usually take a break before I cut on my project. I want a fresh mind so I can pay attention to detail. Once you cut your fabric during this sizing process, there are no "do overs." I am always happy to take these extra steps to be safe rather than sorry.

What about edges that are irregular or rounded shapes or have parts of the design coming off the edges? The same general sizing recommendations apply to ensure your piece lays flat with no ripples in it.

### *Edge Finishing Tips*

I am amazed at the creativity used for edge treatments in fiber creations. The edge-finishing technique can add tremendously to the finished product. There are so many different options to creating the edges. There are great resources on the internet, as well as books and magazine articles covering this topic.

I have used several different techniques and I have my favorites, depending on the subject matter of my piece or the entry requirements. The choice of the edge-finishing technique is personal, and should reflect your own creative voice. Here are my tips:

- Consider how you plan to hang or display the piece. More details in the next section. When you think about how to finish your edges, also consider how the piece will be displayed. That may affect your edging technique decision.

- Plan - at least before you trim your piece. This was mentioned earlier in this section; it is only important if your finished project size must be precise (a particular size). Depending on the edge finish option you choose, the cut size of your trimmed piece may be different. Some edge-finishing techniques require turning a portion of the edge to the back. That will change the finished size unless it is factored in. Other techniques may add bulk to the edge, also changing the finished size. The size difference may not be much, but it could make an impact, especially if the goal is to hang projects side-by-side or fit them together somehow.

- Be creative! Have fun! Think about the message you want to communicate and what your subject matter is. The colors and the materials you use in your edging

speaks volumes, along with all the other aspects of your finished piece.

### *Considerations for Hanging Your Piece - Tips*

Where and how will your project be displayed? If you are planning to enter it into a show, there may be very specific requirements for hanging the piece. Each show may have different requirements. For example, a quilt show may require the use of a fabric sleeve on the back. A gallery show may require that the piece already have a hanging wire attached to it, making it ready to hang.

Also consider how you will get the piece to a gallery or show. If you cannot hand-deliver it, you will have to ship or mail it. Your chosen hanging/displaying method may make shipping more difficult or expensive. Consider these things early in your planning and design stages.

Each show may have different requirements for displaying your project, so your choice may limit where you can show it. There are many options, including:

- Fabric sleeve - One long sleeve across the back of the piece, or a series of shorter sleeves to provide flexibility for hanging options

- Hanging or corner tabs, either visible or on the back

- Hanging support items that are incorporated into the design of the piece and support the piece when hung for display (e.g., tree limbs and other items that become part of the piece itself).

- Mounted project - Securing the piece, either permanently or temporarily, to a physical frame that has a hanging wire; a stretcher frame, stretched canvas, or wood panel; surface mount the piece, painting the edges of the frame or wrapping it with fabric, either using the edges of your piece or separate fabric

- Framed project - A picture frame or shadow box frame, with the piece

mounted inside, either with or without a mat, and with or without the glass

It is good to consider ways to be flexible with your presentation options. For example, I really like the look of my work when it is displayed-mounted on a canvas or panel, but I also want to have a sleeve on the back to enter it into other exhibitions. Figure out how to support both.

### *Adding the Finishing Touches for Your Piece - Tips*

Here are some recommendations and tips for some finishing touches you might consider adding to your piece. This is the stage where most of your quilting or stitching is complete. There may be some special finishing aspects to consider, but you waited until now to do them. These could include:

- <u>Adding highlights</u> using pigments - add final highlights to the piece; reinforce the layers of pigment colors that may have been affected by handling of the piece; if you "touch up" your pigments, try to set them or use a medium to protect them (painted or sprayed on the surface)

- <u>Adding embellishments</u> - beads, other surface design items, special embroidery stitching, as well as items that need to be attached using glues or other means to secure them, can be done now; wait until pigments have been touched up before doing this

- <u>Your label</u> - you should always label your projects; minimally, include your name and the name of your piece, as well as your address and contact information (in case the piece is lost in transit so there is a better chance that it can be returned to you); research for examples and other ideas of information to include on the label
  You might consider using a creative label on your piece, not just a rectangular piece of fabric with writing on it; perhaps in a

shape tying the front and back together; use your imagination and have fun

- <u>Your signature or mark</u> - always add your signature, mark, symbol, or special characters; make sure it doesn't get cut off during the trimming process or covered up by the edging method; use pigments to write your name or signature, or use stitching; be proud of what you create and put your name on it for all to see.

- <u>Add a special touch or surprise</u> - add something special as a surprise; a fun embellishment, extra pieces from your project, etc.; add some appeal to the back of your piece; consider it a treat for whoever looks at the quilt back

## Summary - Finishing Your Project

You now understand some of the things to consider when finishing your project, especially since you used Pigment Patchwork techniques to create it. Observing these tips and recommendations, and abiding by them, will ensure that all your creative efforts will be enhanced and supported during the process of finishing your project.

GREYHOUND

# Some Final Thoughts & Words of Wisdom

## Some Final Thoughts & Words of Wisdom

### Your Creative Voice - What Is It?

In her article, "What is an Artist's Voice and How to Find It" Leni Levenson Wiener, author of several articles about your creative voice on the website weallsew.com, defines your creative voice as:

> "...a unique and recognizable artistic style that is distinctly your own; your inspiration, your materials, techniques, themes, and color palette all working together in a way that looks like it comes from you and no one else."

We all have a creative voice, whether it is expressing your message using fiber art or any other endeavor where you are creating something.

### Your Creative Voice - How to Find It

Leni goes on to say that you just need to find your voice. She says, "Many artists grapple with finding their voice, but most don't realize their voice is there from the beginning, they just need to hear it and follow it."

You can develop your creative voice, honing and tuning it, with knowledge of different techniques, experimentation, and testing. With this book, you've been introduced to my Pigment Patchwork techniques. The Learning Activities gave you an opportunity to experiment and create projects using pigments on fabric. Hopefully, this is just the beginning of your adventures.

Pigment Patchwork is a set of tools (techniques) to help you on your journey to refine your creative voice. The more you play and experiment using pigments on fabric, the more you can refine your own techniques using them. You are exploring with your creative voice, honing your skills. I am very glad to have been part of that.

I hope that you continue, and I would love to continue to be part of your journey.

Thank you!

### Where to Now?

If you liked learning about coloring on fabric and using the activities in this book, then I hope that you are hungry for more!

I purposely did not include step-by-step instructions for coloring a specific project. I did share some photographs of samples and some in-progress examples, but that was all. I did that for a reason. Had I shown you how I do things, my step-by-step process, you would have lost the opportunity for discovery on your own. That is so important for learning, and I wanted to be sure you experienced all the things that might happen when asked to do tasks and projects using pigments on fabric.

To use an analogy, I am teaching you how to fish. Now that you have that exposure and a better understanding of what happens, your initiation is complete. You should never be intimidated by any new pigment you encounter. Congratulations!

The best way to continue developing your confidence and skills is to practice and experiment. Each time you do that, you expand your experience base and gain insights into refining your own creative voice. Use the approaches you've learned to grow your knowledge by expanding to other pigments and other fabrics. The possibilities are infinite.

If you want guided learning opportunities with me, I offer in-person workshops, on-line workshops, or on-demand classes, as well as mentoring opportunities. I am continuously working to provide learning opportunities in different formats to support those interested in working with me to develop their skills.

Details of my offerings are on my website, RhondaDenney.com. You can see my portfolio of fiber art and look at my blog. You can sign up for my Newsletters. You can join my Pigment Patchwork Mastery Community, a group of like-minded people who support each other along their creative journeys. You can also schedule a free call with me to talk about your goals and we can brainstorm ideas on possible strategies for your continued growth. I am always interested in ideas for topics for training and mentoring, so please contact me through my website with your thoughts.

You now have the tools (the concepts and techniques that I use) to continue your own journey. Hopefully you will never feel daunted by a pigment again! You know the proper approach to learn to "dance with the pigments" and work with them to create magic in your creative voice. You are a Pigment Trailblazer!

### Final Words of Wisdom

Please don't forget some of my words of wisdom shared in this book:

- Give yourself permission to play
- Be patient and kind with yourself and your learning progress
- Embrace the wicking!
- Dance with the pigment!
- Practice makes progress!

I wish you all the best with your creative voice enrichment journey!  Take care!

Enthusiastically,

*Rhonda S. Denney*

www.RhondaDenney.com

Pigment Patchwork

Rhonda's Inspirational Quote -
Pigment Patchwork

"Give yourself permission to play!  Try something new and different! You may make mistakes, but those are simply learning experiences.  And, you may find that you like what you created!  If nothing else, you have learned a valuable lesson."





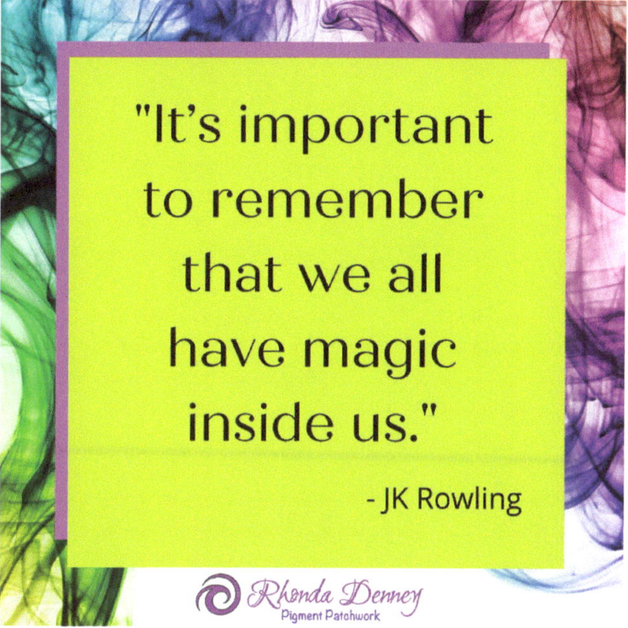

NATURE'S
SYMPHONY

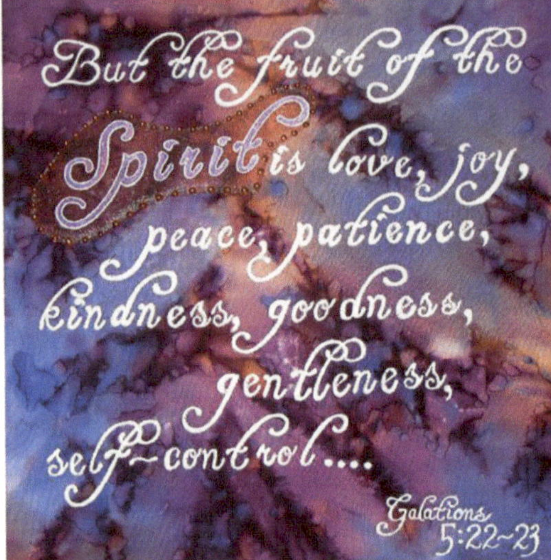
But the fruit of the
Spirit is love, joy,
peace, patience,
kindness, goodness,
gentleness,
self-control....
Galatians
5:22-23

Celebrate

## Highlights of Some of Rhonda's Work

Throughout this book, some of my comments and teachings were illustrated using detailed photos of my work. I thought it would be encouraging to give you a broader view of some of those projects. My focus is to represent the variety of projects you can do, the subject matter that can be used, and a high-level overview of the progression from start to finish. I will explain what I did and why, as well as the pigments I used. I hope you enjoy these.

There are five projects. You have seen all of them, in some form, in this book.

- Zebra - The Eyes Have It
- Hans my Hedgehog
- Buzzing with Bees, How Sweet it Is
- Rabbit - Winter Early Morning Light
- Rub-a-dub-dub – Pieces of the Past

## Zebra - The Eyes Have It (TEHI)

This is a whole-cloth piece, created on silk noil (raw silk). Silk noil is a wonderful fabric on which to color because of its nubby surface and natural off-white color with random dark flecks. The finished size of this project is 40" x 30". The following pictures show the progression of the coloring on the fabric and the final product.

### Zebra - The Eyes Have It - 1

This is my piece of silk noil, ironed onto freezer paper, with the pattern transferred to the front. You can see the edge of my reference photograph on the left. I was using a large table to work on.

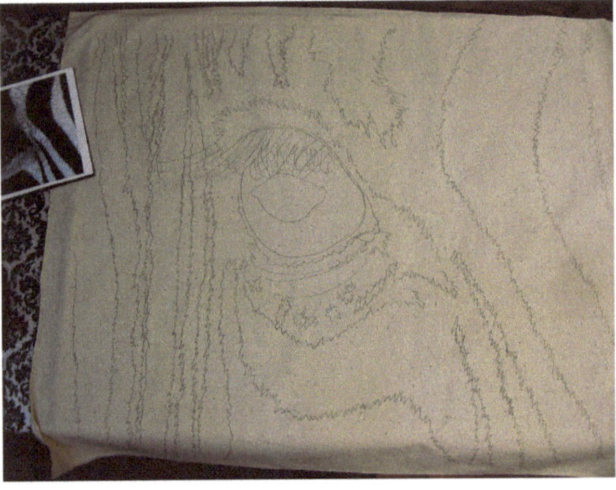

### Zebra - The Eyes Have It - 2

This is the zebra in progress. I darkened my lines and am starting to fill in areas. For this

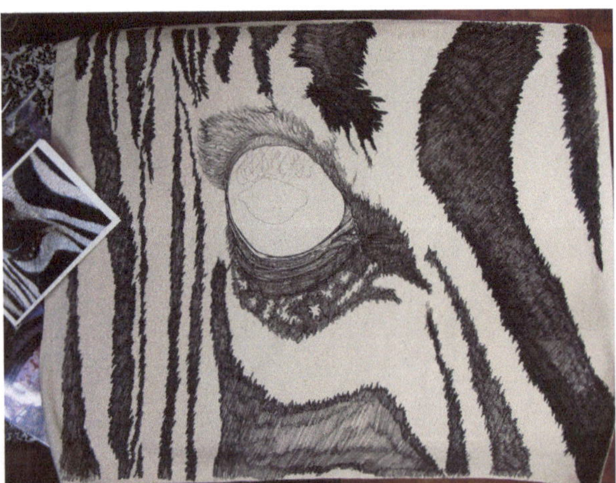

piece I used a Sharpie black marker. I wanted to emphasize the hair, especially since this is a close-up view of the zebra's face. The medium tip on the black marker worked well. My pen strokes resemble the hair on the zebra's hide, the strokes made in the same direction as the hair naturally grew. I added the pigment using layers, adding texture and realism. I used the silk noil fabric as my white color in the composition, except for the highlights.

### Zebra - The Eyes Have It - 3

Here I continue adding pigment in strokes, darkening the black in the zebra's stripes.

### Zebra - The Eyes Have It - 4

This photograph shows most of the black stripes completed. I started adding color to the eye of the zebra, keeping the reflection area free of pigments to keep the light color.

### *Zebra - The Eyes Have It* - 5

Here is the finished top, ready for sandwiching and quilting. I will add more pigment after the quilting process.

### *Zebra - The Eyes Have It* - 6

This is the quilted piece. I sandwiched the piece using a low-loft polyester batting. I used a clear monofilament thread to free-motion stitch this project. My stitching was very dense and directional to look like hair on the face of the zebra. I quilted over the entire piece. There was no pigment on the white zebra stripes. The stitching represented the hair throughout and tied everything together.

### *Zebra - The Eyes Have It* - Finished

After the quilting I added the long guard hairs at the eye. The piece was trimmed and edged using a rat-tail binding technique and then permanently mounted to a painted wood panel.

### *Zebra - The Eyes Have It* - With Artist

The artist beside the finished, mounted piece, illustrating how large the piece is and how dramatic the close-up of the zebra looks.

### Hans my Hedgehog

The second project in my review is called *Hans-my-Hedgehog*. There was a Call for Entry titled "Once Upon a Time - Grimmly Inspired," sponsored by the Edsel Ford Company, Chicago, IL. We were offered a list of lesser known Grimms Fairy Tales from which to choose. The task was to create art inspired by the story of our choosing. I decided on the story "Hans my Hedgehog" and designed my image based on my interpretation of highlights in the story. It shows Hans, a fictional part-boy-part-hedgehog storybook character, playing his bagpipes while riding his shod cock-rooster.

This is another whole-cloth piece for which I used black cotton as my fabric base. I wanted to see how well pigments would show up on the black fabric. This piece was created using color pencils, pastels, and gel pens. The finished size of this project is 22" x 32". The following pictures show the progression of the coloring-on-fabric process.

### Hans my Hedgehog - 1

This first picture is a close-up of my piece of black cotton, ironed onto freezer paper, with the pattern transferred to the front.

It was a challenge to get the pattern transferred to the black fabric. My homemade light box was not powerful enough for me to see the lines through the black fabric. So, I used my large window on a bright sunny day. I drew the pattern lines in white, knowing I would cover them up with pigments as I developed the drawing. I've already started adding color to the black fabric in this picture. I am developing my design, darkening the colors using layers. I used paper to protect the colored surface so I would not lay my hand in the pigment.

### Hans my Hedgehog - 2

Here I am continuing to develop my design, darkening the colors using layers, using paper underneath my hand as I colored. This is one of my best practices for protecting the colored surface and protecting the coloring hand.

### *Hans my Hedgehog* - 3

Progress on my coloring continues. I focused on coloring Hans first. You can see that I start with the lighter colors first, then develop the dimension using darker colors. It is easier to darken the colors on top of a light base. It would be more challenging to do it the other way around, and probably not as successful.

### *Hans my Hedgehog* - 4

In this next photo, I am coloring the rooster, adding his shod feet and starting on his tail. I am waiting to do the other wing until I develop the coloring for the rooster's body. I use the black fabric base to help define the feathers, leaving space around my white color pencil strokes. This way I may only need to use a black pigment as a highlighter in areas. I love how the colors "pop" on the black fabric, making them look richer. Using layers is key.

### *Hans my Hedgehog* - 5

This is the finished top, with most of the coloring complete except for any highlights. This piece is now ready to sandwich/layer and stitch.

### *Hans my Hedgehog* - 6

This next photo is lit to show the free motion stitching I did. The next step will be to do some final touch-ups using my pigments.

### *Hans my Hedgehog* - **Finished**

This last picture is the finished piece. I really enjoyed this project. It had a lot of "firsts" for me regarding coloring on fabric. I am always experimenting with the use of pigments on fabric.

## How Sweet It Is ... Buzzing with Bees

This is the third project in my review. This one is called *How Sweet It Is . . . Buzzing with Bees*. This Call- for-Entry theme required bees in it. I used a photograph of a friend's daughter looking at some flowers and imagined her sharing the blooms with the bees. The finished project is 34" x 25'. This is an appliqué piece, using both turned-edge and raw-edge appliqué. The following pictures show the progression of the coloring on fabric process.

### How Sweet It Is . . . Buzzing with Bees - 1

This first photograph shows the muslin fabric I used for the base of my girl, ironed onto freezer paper to stabilize it. The pattern of the girl was transferred to the fabric, and I colored her flesh using a combination of alcohol inks, color pencils, and pastels.

In this photo I am continuing to add pigment color.

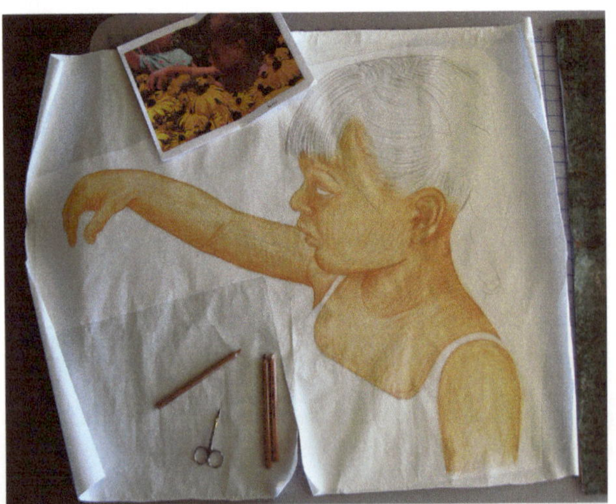

### How Sweet It Is . . . Buzzing with Bees - 2

This photograph shows the girl's hair in progress.

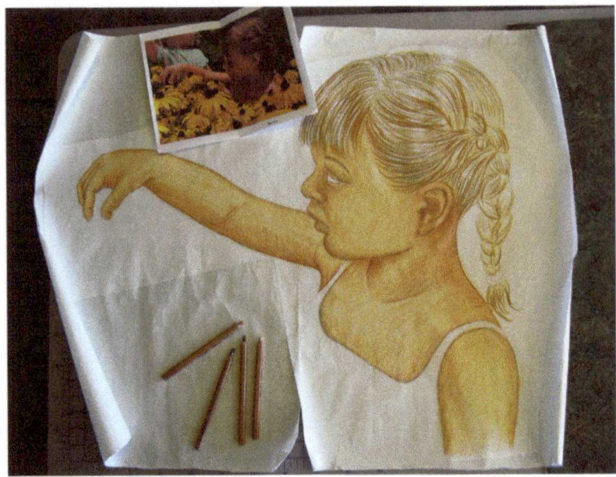

I used organza fabrics because of their translucent properties. I had fun developing the colors and depth in her hair by using pigments and the fabrics together. Layers of different colored organza fabric helped create the effect. You can see the dark pigments underneath and on top of the sheer fabric. Stitching using colored threads helped tie it all together.

I used stitching to create portions of this appliqué unit before it was added to my background fabric. This meant I would only have to quilt supporting stitches to secure it and add dimension.

### *How Sweet It Is . . . Buzzing with Bees* - 3

In this next picture you can see the resulting appliqué of the girl. Her dress has been added to the fleshtone piece, making it a complete appliqué unit. The dress is turned-edge appliqué. I already stitched the dress down onto the girl's body to keep it secure. The girl is trimmed with a ¼" edge of fabric around the skin portions of her body. Her hair was trimmed without an edge so I could use raw-edge appliqué for that portion. She is laying on top of the background. This shows that you can combine different appliqué techniques in one unit. I also added a backing fabric to the girl because I was concerned about potential shadowing from the dark-green background.

The background has already been sandwiched and quilted for this project. I did not want to try to quilt the background around all the flower appliqués, so I marked where the girl would be and quilted around the other parts of the quilt before I added the girl and the flowers.

### *How Sweet It Is . . . Buzzing with Bees* - 4

This next picture shows the girl sewn down on the edges to secure her in place. The turned-edge appliqué method I used gave me a nice, clean edge for her skin and the dress. If you look closely, there are parts of her that have not been sewn down yet (look at her hand near the flowers - you can see the fabric edge for my turned-edge appliqué method still showing).

Some flowers were added as I developed the layers for perspective. I want some flowers behind her hand, and she is pinching the cone of the black-eyed Susan flower, so her finger will be behind the flower cone and her thumb in front of it. Leaving her hand unstitched will allow me to layer. Some flowers will overlap parts of her body. Future layers of fabric pieces will create that effect.

I used a variety of different fabrics to create the flowers including organza, batiks, sheers, etc. I used velvet and other interesting black fabrics for the flower cones. It was fun experimenting with the look of them in the piece. The flowers (and her fingers) were stitched down as I built my design to keep them in position. More quilting stitches will be added later.

### *How Sweet It Is . . . Buzzing with Bees* - 5

In this photograph, all the flowers have been added and stitched down. You can see the extra "real estate" of fabric around the edge of my project (the applique does not go all the way to the edge of the background fabric). This will provide me with a narrow travel corridor for my stitching when that time comes. Then I can cut it away during the final trimming.

### *How Sweet It Is . . . Buzzing with Bees* - 6

This picture shows the quilting that has been done on the flowers and the girl to add definition and dimension. There is still more free-motion quilting to do.

### *How Sweet It Is . . . Buzzing with Bees* - **Finished**

This is the finished piece. The quilting has been completed. You can see some of the stitching on the girl's face. I added more pigment to her face to darken and add highlights. I usually add stitching much as I do my pigments–using layers and, after seeing the effect, adding more stitching if needed.  This gives me flexibility in my design process.

The bees were added last, after all the sewing was complete. The bees are embellishments (3-D stickers).

## *Rabbit - Winter Early Morning Light*

This is the fourth project in my review. This one is called *Rabbit - Winter Early Morning Light*. The inspiration photograph was one I took outside our window at the ranch on a very coldwinter morning. The rabbit was all fluffed up to stay warm, sitting to absorb the sun's early morning rays. The finished project is 12" x 12". This is an appliqué piece, using both reverse appliqué and raw-edge appliqué . The following pictures show the progression of the coloring-on-fabric process.

## *Rabbit - Winter Early Morning Light - 1*

This first photograph shows the reverse appliqué fused onto the background fabric and sandwiched, ready for stitching to secure the edges. I stitched the edges down before I colored, wanting to be sure my coloring process would not cause the fabric to separate. You can see some of my pattern lines, drawn using a light-blue line. You can see the shadowing effect from the dark-brown fabric ironed behind the lighter foreground. That was okay because I wanted the snow to look light enough to see some rock under it.

## *Rabbit - Winter Early Morning Light - 2*

This photograph shows the stitching securing the edges of the reverse appliqué, as well as the pigments I used to highlight and add shadows to the snow and rocks. I used alcohol ink markers and gel pens. The uncolored shape is where my appliqué for the rabbit will go. I was careful to extend my coloring into the inside edges of the shape where the rabbit will go. Applying the pigment beforehand helps make the color smooth; it will be behind the appliqué piece.

## *Rabbit - Winter Early Morning Light - 3*

This next picture is the rabbit appliqué piece I created. I used color pencils and gel pens on this fabric. The brown fabric gave me a nice base for my pigments.

Notice I left myself plenty of fabric around the edges. Edges will be trimmed (for raw-edge appliqué) once the coloring is done and the rabbit is ready to be stitched to the background.

### *Rabbit - Winter Early Morning Light* - 4

The trimmed rabbit appliqué is stitched to the piece, and quilting added for dimension and texture. It is ready for trimming and finishing.

### *Rabbit - Winter Early Morning Light* - **Finished**

Here is the finished Rabbit - Winter Early Morning Light piece, with a turned-edge artist facing.

## Rub-a-dub-dub – Pieces of the Past

This is the fifth and final project in my review. This one is called *Rub-a-dub-dub – Pieces of the Past*. The inspiration photograph was an old, faded-color family snapshot, shown here.

My mother is with my little sister. The remaining five kids (including me) are in a metal water trough we ran across alongside a river in Colorado on one of our road trips. I loved the picture and it fit the theme "Pieces of the Past." The finished project is 24" x 30". This is an appliqué piece using raw-edge appliqué.

The following pictures show the progression of the coloring-on-fabric process. I was able to include more photographs showing details of my progression because I planned and took the time to take pictures along the way. This is another of my best practices.

### Rub-a-dub-dub - 1

This first photograph shows the reverse pattern lines drawn on paper-backed iron-on fusible and cut out. You can see the extra fusible left around the pattern for later trimming. Until I know what appliqué technique I will use, I want to give myself extra fabric to keep my options open. And, the extra fusible helps hold the edges of the fabric so, when I do cut the pieces out, the edges are less likely to fray.

### Rub-a-dub-dub - 2

Here are the fusible pattern pieces ironed to the backside of my flesh-tone base fabric, leaving extra space around the pieces.

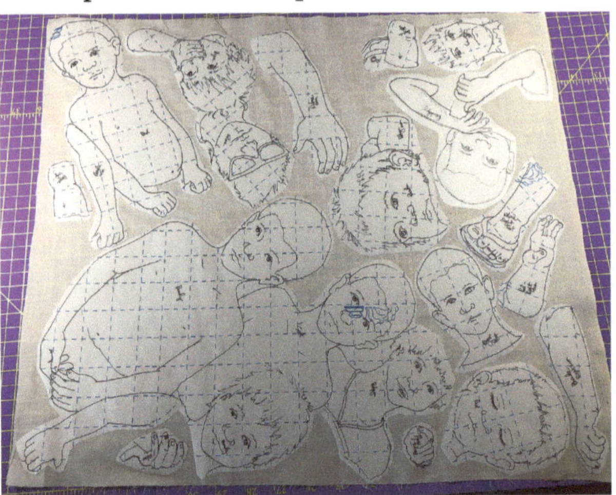

### Rub-a-dub-dub - 3

This is the front of the fabric, with key guidelines transferred to the fabric using a tan color pencil. These lines will be covered by my coloring process.

### Rub-a-dub-dub - 4

I kept the fabric piece whole to start with. Using layers of pigment and wet medium, I start by developing the base layer for one of the kids' bodies on the fabric. I used Inktense and aloe to give me the blending of the skin-tone colors. Later I would use color pencils to define details.

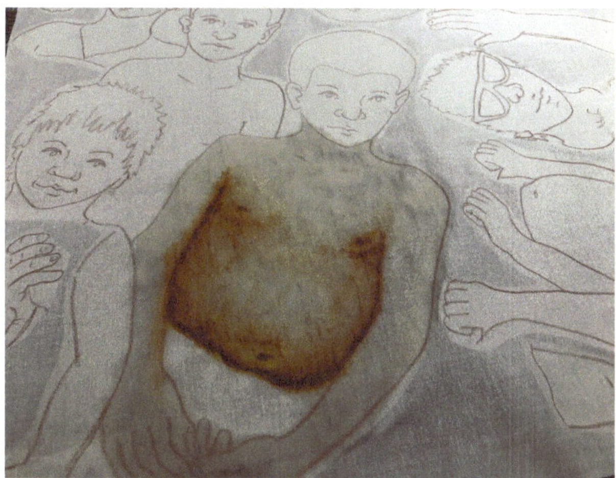

You can see where the pigment has extended beyond the outline of the arm on the right. I was being more careful about that on the left arm because of the other bodies that are part of this appliqué piece.

### Rub-a-dub-dub - 5

Here you can see the flesh-tone wash on my pieces, and some details added using dry pigments. The pieces are cut apart now, leaving piece groupings together, with extra fabric around the edges. You can also see that my coloring has extended outside my outlines. More detail will be added using color pencils, layering the pigments.

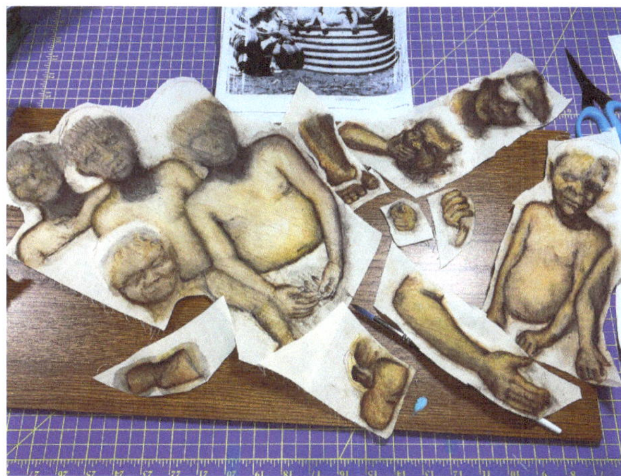

### Rub-a-dub-dub - 6

Details are added to the faces and bodies and the appliqué pieces have been trimmed, still leaving a ¼" edge around them.

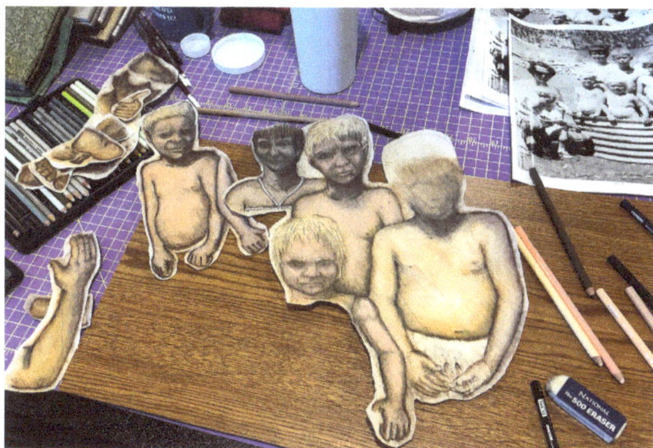

### Rub-a-dub-dub - 7

I used my master pattern to create the fabric pieces for the water trough. I will use fabric to help create the dimensions, with pigment added for more detail and blending. You can see my lightbox that I am using to draw my guidelines on the front of the fabric.

### Rub-a-dub-dub - 8

The water trough appliqué piece is ready to add. It will be raw-edge appliqué, so the edges have been trimmed to their final size. More pigments can be added later for more detail.

### *Rub-a-dub-dub* - 9

I created my master layout guidelines on my base muslin fabric. This fabric base is important because my background will be composed of many different fabrics and I need a way to secure them.

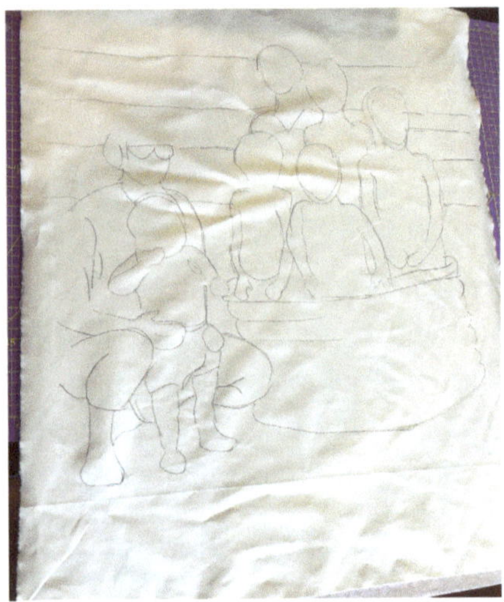

### *Rub-a-dub-dub* - 10

Using the ready appliqué pieces, I start to think about the background. I auditioned several different fabrics, trying to determine the best ones to help develop the perspective I wanted. This set of fabrics does not make the final cut; you will see what I chose for the background in later pictures.

### *Rub-a-dub-dub* - 11

Here is the appliqué unit of the people and the water trough. Having decided to use raw-edge appliqué, the edges are trimmed to their final size and the pieces fused together with the iron. The unit is laying on a piece of muslin to show the cut edge details.

### *Rub-a-dub-dub* - 12

Using my appliqué unit to gauge the look, my background fabric decisions are finalized. The next step will be to secure the fabric pieces to my base muslin, and sew to secure the edges of all the background fabrics before I add my appliqué unit.

### *Rub-a-dub-dub* - 13

In this picture, I am working on more pigment details, using color pencils. Having the appliqué  laying on the background is helpful in determining the right colors to use, as well as thinking about how I will use pigments to develop details in the foreground. I want to do some initial quilting on the background portion before I secure the appliqué piece, so my stitching will be underneath the appliqué.

### *Rub-a-dub-dub* - 14

Here you can see the water trough area marked (the pigments also represent the shadows I will develop further), so I know roughly where the appliqué will sit in the background. This allows me to quilt around the edges of that location before I fuse my appliqué to the background.

### *Rub-a-dub-dub* - 15

After quilting the fused appliqué units to secure them, I start using my stitches to add dimension and definition.

### *Rub-a-dub-dub* - 16

Using pigments, I add details to the foreground and touch up areas as needed. The sandwiched piece is now ready for a final trim.

### *Rub-a-dub-dub* - 17

The edges are finished using an artist's facing edge. The next steps include adding a hanging sleeve and label. Pigment highlights will also be added.

### *Rub-a-dub-dub* - Finished

And here is the finished piece.

### Summary - Highlights of Some of Rhonda's Work

I hope these projects have inspired you to try your hand at more Pigment Patchwork projects. I am sure the confidence you've gained from your experiences with the book assignments will continue to carry you further.

Remember, the more you allow yourself to play and explore using pigments on fabric, the greater your confidence will be. You can use patterns or create your own designs from photographs or create them free-form if you like. If you are interested in learning more about my Pigment Patchwork techniques, please contact me through my website, RhondaDenney.com.

> ❝
> A willingness to experiment using different techniques and methods of creation, learning as you go
>
> What is Pigment Patchwork?
>
> Rhonda Denney

We have
only today.
Let us begin.

# Resources

## Templates, Patterns and Reference Materials

This section contains the patterns and any associated reference materials for the Learning Activities. Please make a copy of the line patterns for use. You can either make copies of the reference materials or refer to them in the book.

The materials are outlined in this section, with thumbnail photographs. The full-size materials are in their own sections following the same order as they are presented here.

### *Butterflies Line Pattern - 2 patterns to a page Overview*

This Butterflies pattern is used for the coloring assignment in Part 2 - Getting Acquainted - Let's Color! Instructions for the use of this pattern are contained there.

### *Test Sheet Templates - Generic Overview*

These Test Sheet Templates patterns are used for the coloring assignments in Part 4 - Techniques and

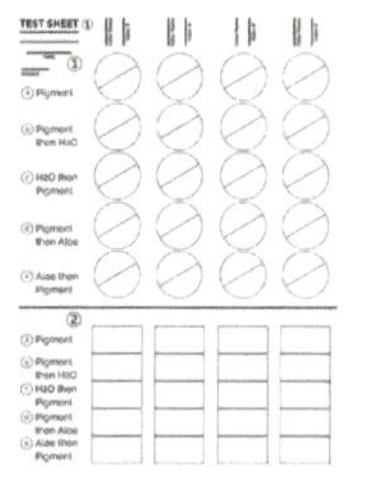

Tools - A Workbook. Instructions for the use of these templates are included there.

### *Koi Fish Line Pattern and Reference Materials - Overview*

This Koi Fish pattern and reference materials are used for the coloring assignments starting in Part 4 - Techniques and

Tools - A Workbook. Instructions for the use of this pattern are outlined there.

### *Deer Portrait Line Pattern and Reference Materials - Overview*

This Deer Portrait pattern and reference materials are used for the coloring assignments starting in Part 4 - Techniques and Tools - A Workbook. Instructions for the use of this pattern are contained there.

### *Color Wheel Reference Materials - Overview*

This color-wheel diagram is included in this Resources section. It shows a CMYK/RGB Color Wheel. Details are contained in Part 3 - Essential Elements - Pigments and Fabric.

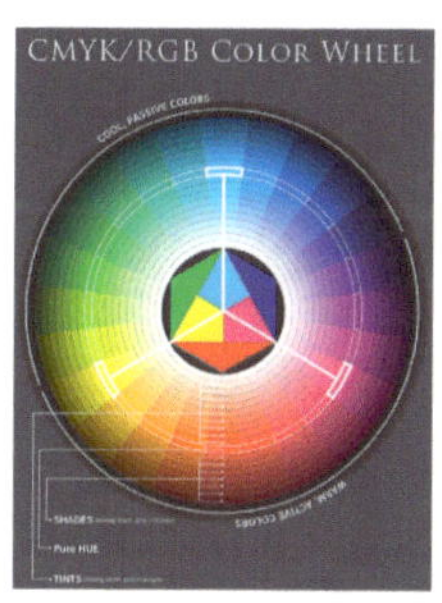

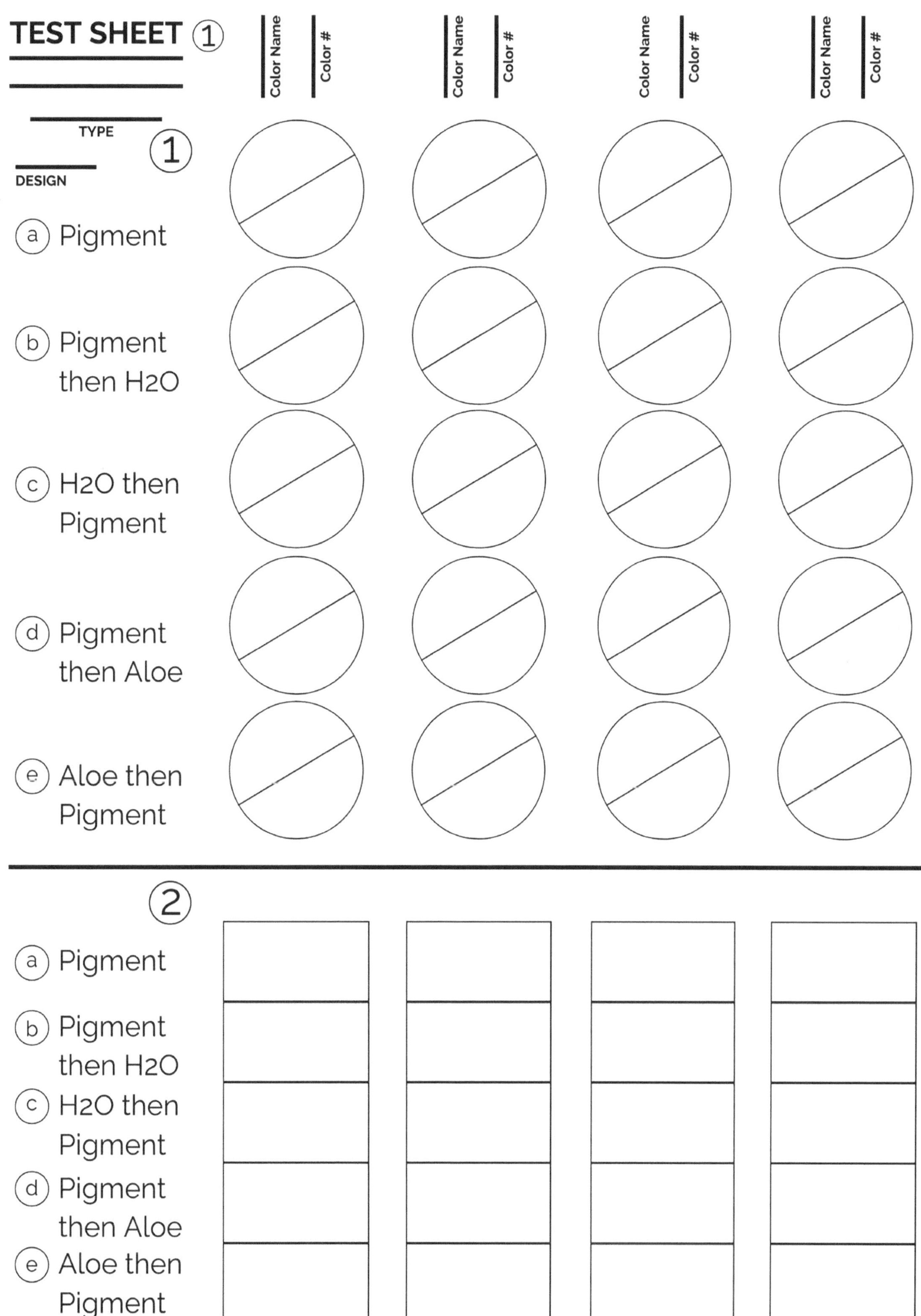

TEST SHEET ①

TYPE
DESIGN

① 
Color Name | Color #
Color Name | Color #
Color Name | Color #
Color Name | Color #

a Pigment
b Pigment then H2O
c H2O then Pigment
d Pigment then Aloe
e Aloe then Pigment

②
a Pigment
b Pigment then H2O
c H2O then Pigment
d Pigment then Aloe
e Aloe then Pigment

# TEST SHEET ③

TYPE

DESIGN

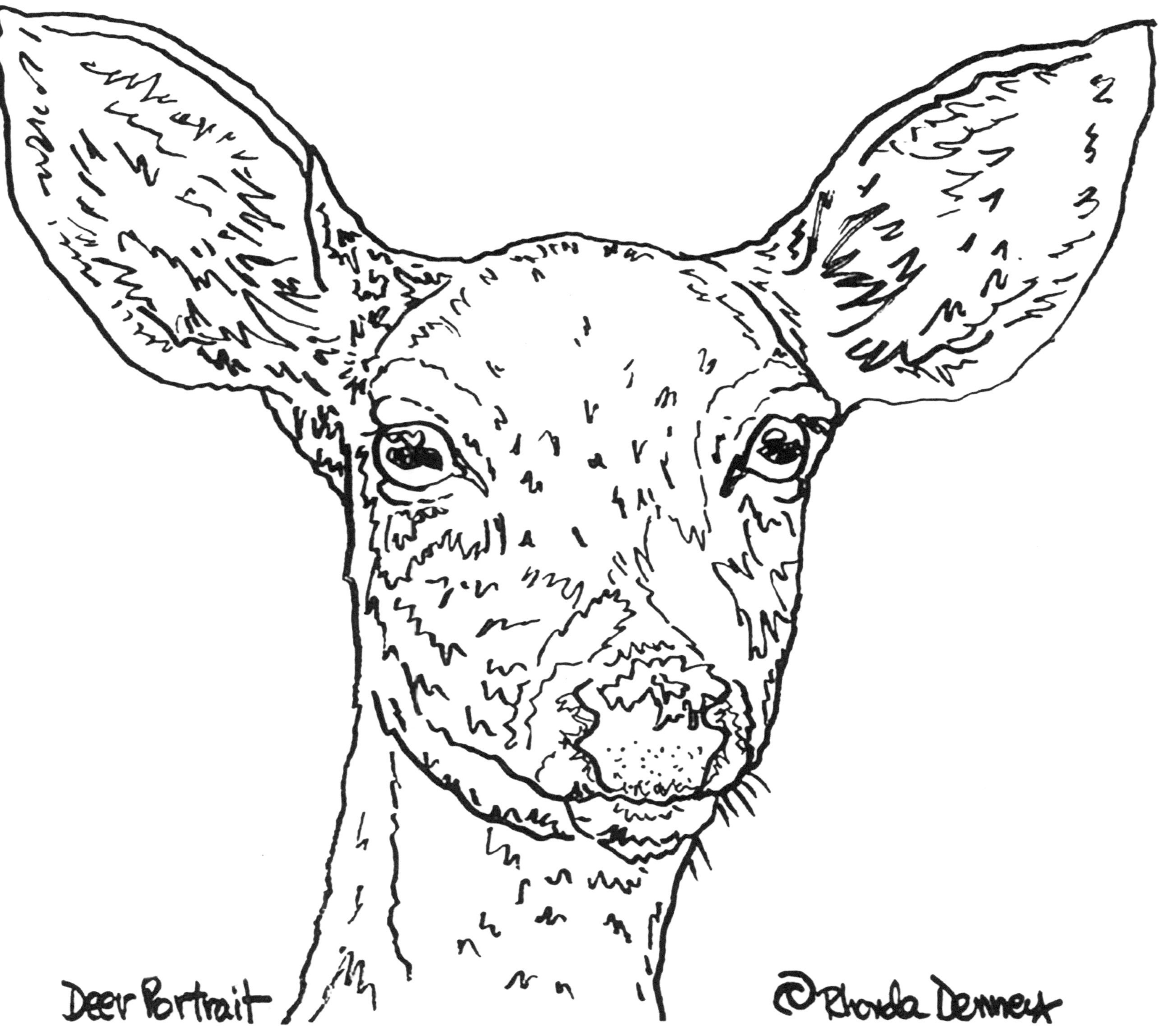
Deer Portrait
©Rhonda Dennert

# CMYK/RGB Color Wheel

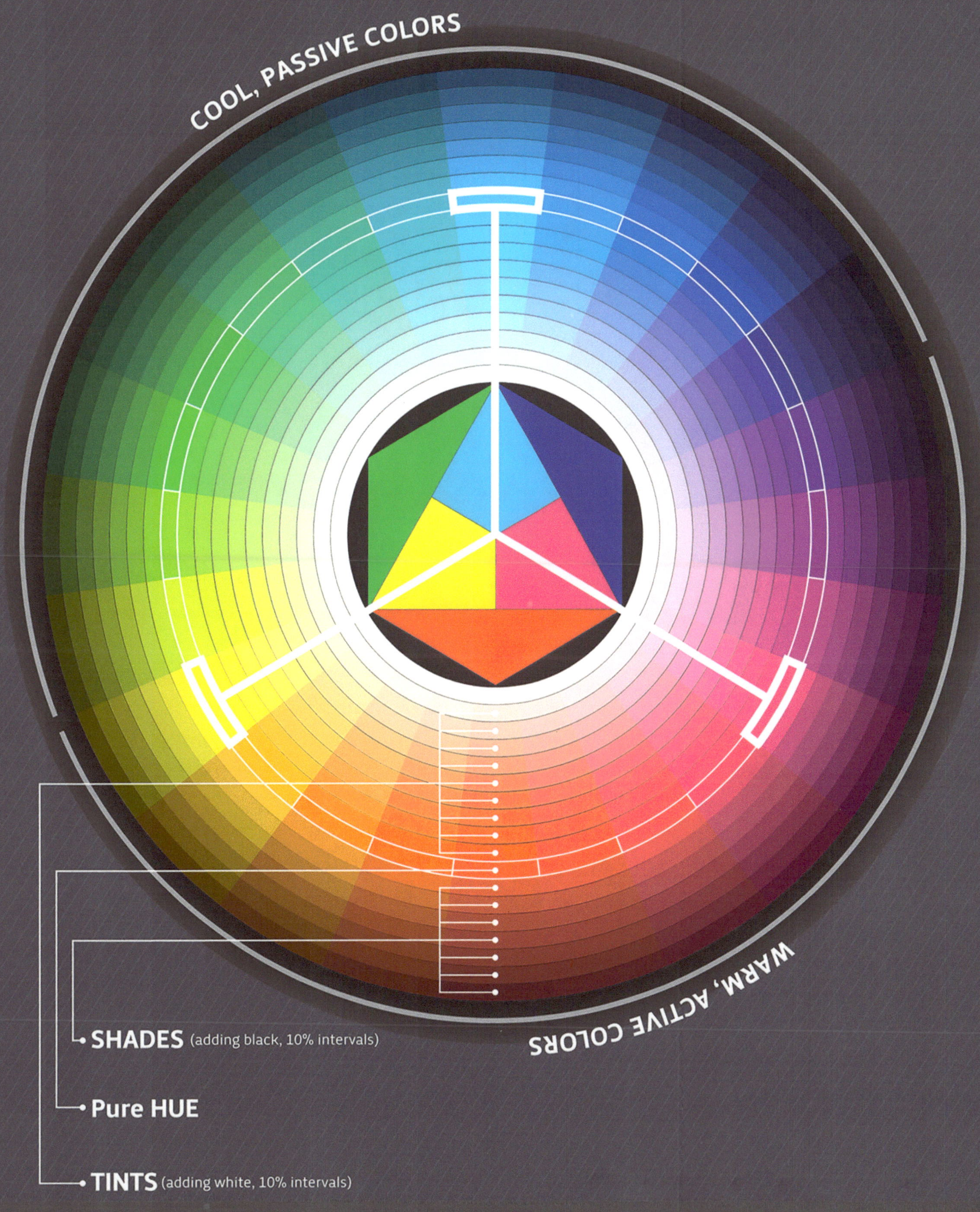

# COLOR THEORY

## CMYK/RGB Color Wheel

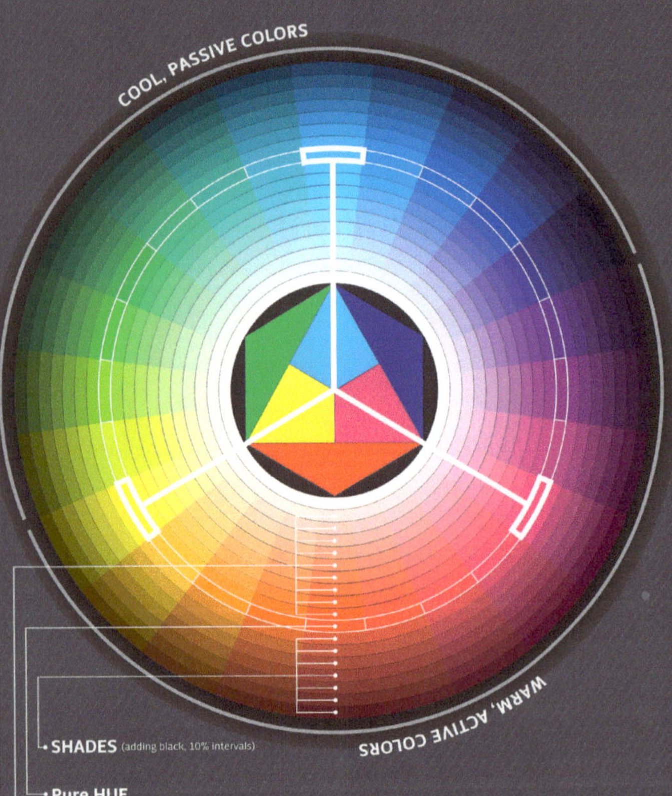


## Color Systems

## Color Types

**Primary**
RED, YELLOW, BLUE
Colors that can not be mixed. All other colors are derived from these 3 hues.

**Secondary**
GREEN, ORANGE, PURPLE
Colors formed by mixing the primary colors.

**Tertiary**
YELLOW-ORANGE, RED-ORANGE, RED-PURPLE, BLUE-PURPLE, BLUE-GREEN, YELLOW-GREEN
colors formed by mixing a primary and a secondary color.

**Complementary**
Colors that are opposite each other on the color wheel.

**Analogous**
Analogous color schemes use colors that are next to each other on the color wheel.

## Classic Color Schemes

**Monochromatic**
The monochromatic color scheme uses variations in lightness and saturation of a single color.

**Analogous**
The analogous color schemes use colors that are next to each other on the color wheel.

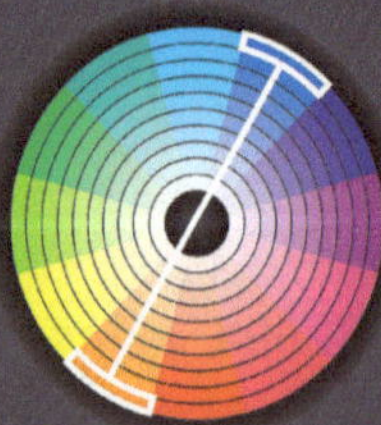
**Complementary**
The complementary color scheme use colors that are opposite each other on the color wheel.

**Split complementary**
The split-complementary color scheme is a variation of the complementary color scheme. In addition to the base color, it uses the two colors adjacent to its complement.

**Double-Complementary**
The rectangle or tetradic color scheme uses four colors arranged into two complementary pairs.

**Triadic**
The triadic color scheme uses colors that are evenly spaced around the color wheel

www.ingramcontent.com/pod-product-compliance
Lightning Source LLC
Chambersburg PA
CBHW042148030726
47599CB00004B/653